A Good Son

Breaking Cultural and Generational Trauma

Jonathan Ibrahim

ISBN: 979-8-89663-820-9

Dedication

George Ibrahim 1950 – 2024

This book is dedicated to my father, George Ibrahim. Now I know it seems a little strange, how is it that I'm writing a book about some of the errors that my parents made and dedicated to my father. But the truth of the matter is that my father was an amazing human being. His story started back in the 70s when he came into the United States at 27 years old with not much money in his pocket, inability to speak English and did not have his own place to live. He was truly a self-made man. After years of assimilating to the American culture but still holding true to his Lebanese heritage he met my mom and shortly after I got married and they were pregnant with me and my brother. He lived for his family, ensuring that they had every means necessary to live a comfortable life. He was a man who didn't always speak much but when he spoke people listened. He has gone through many trials and tribulations as an immigrant and set the bar for what we classically known as the American dream. He taught me very valuable lessons about work ethic, honesty, integrity while also teaching me that trust is always earned and should never be expected. In his later years at 73 years old he was diagnosed with Acute Myeloid Leukemia, also known as AML. As stubborn as the man was with every health issue he's ever faced, this was the first time where he blindly followed everyone who shared an interest in his well-being. He fought through painstaking chemotherapy, multiple doctor visits and blood transfusions for a year where he was finally told he was in remission and was preparing for a stem cell transplant in which he'd be receiving stem cells from me. As was getting a cancer diagnosis was uncharted territory a stem cell transplant would also be a new journey to where we would not be sure of it's outcome. After receiving the stem cell transplant his health started to decline rapidly and on June 20, 2024, George Ibrahim was no longer with us. I dedicate this book to my father who has been a pillar in my life and all of his lessons and love will live forever in my heart.

Acknowledgments

This book was a lot more challenging to write and could not have done it without the help and inspiration from my cousin Cynthia who believed in my so much this book became a reality.

The team at Bestseller Ghostwriting, who helped me get my story on paper.

My friends who have been big supporters through my journey and this experience from start to finish.

About The Author

Jonathan Ibrahim was born on February 7, 1990, in Los Angeles California as part of a set of twins. He is first generation Lebanese American along with his fraternal twin brother. Jonathan grew up in a loving, vibrant home that was rich in Lebanese culture and more extended family than most. There he and his brother were raised by their two parents George and Sandy who poured their love into their family. Jonathan was a more creative child compared to his brother who loved tinkering in the garage, getting his hands dirty. Jonathan loved to color, draw, act and sing, always trying to get the attention of the crowd to showcase his talents. Jonathan also knew that he was different at his young age though he did not understand what it was or was able to place language around his feeling. As he grew up him and his brothers' differences grew. His brother, being popular and had many friends while Jonathan kept more to himself since he was bullied heavily. This became a theme in Jonathan's adolescence through his teen years trying desperately to become the guy everyone wanted to be friends with. He eventually was able to understand why he was different compared to his male peers, but it was a secret as he knew it would create more unwanted attention. Jonathan grew up in a hypermasculine environment and was fearful of rejection from his family for his big secret. To distract from his secret, he kept busy being productive at young age, getting his first job at sixteen years old while attending school and playing sports. His brother became the rebel of the family while

Jonathan acquired the reputation of being the obedient, helpful and a reliable son which eventually caused for a lot of pressure to accommodate his family through his adulthood. After Jonathan had revealed his big secret of being gay to his family his parents were less than happy for him, making him feel as if he was broken for having shared his true identity. This negative experience thrust him into an unexpected journey to regain their love and affection. Amidst his family challenges, Jonathan was able to get his Bachelors degree in Nutrition Sciences, get his certification as a personal trainer and start his new career as a fitness and nutrition coach. Jonathan had a real knack for fitness, getting his first job in 2015 at a luxury gym and to his surprise he was the top grossing and busiest trainer on staff. Through his passion he found further enjoyment lifting heavy things that he started bodybuilding, working with Olympia qualifying bodybuilder Breon Ansley for his very first bodybuilding show, marked the beginning of a new intense passion for fitness. Jonathan had competed and places in over seven bodybuilding shows over the next five years but never received a pro card. Jonathan eventually left the commercial gym industry and went into education. Though he left the gym world behind, his passion for fitness remained strong, finding ways to feed his passion, he eventually was able to build out his very own home gym during one of them most historical pandemics in the world where he would train clients. Jonathan's career took a wild turn as he left education to pursued a new job for a fitness tech company in San Francisco. Not only did he learn about the startup industry but started to learn about himself.

Contents

Chapter 1: What Do We Know?

Almost every single one of us knows what it feels like to be praised by others. Whether it's your neighbor, a random stranger whom you helped cross the road, or just a friend, being appreciated is unmatched, especially when it comes from your parents. Growing up, most of you must have experienced the feeling of pride when you earned the title of "A Good Child" from your parents. Whether you're a sibling, a twin, or an only child, "A Good Child" isn't just a title; it's almost like a badge of honor. For children of immigrant parents, the weight of that title is something most American families don't truly understand. When we're young, we are unaware of the responsibilities that come with this title.

It cannot be reduced to a trivial label your parents just say; it's a complete state of being. While we are young and highly impressionable, the only things that matter to us are the statements of praise and affection that accompany this title. This affection could be in the form of a hug, followed by a soft caress on our cheeks, or a loving gaze into our eyes, either before or after we are reprimanded for minor infractions, conditioning us to seek that loving feeling. While we're receiving all this praise and affection, the levels of dopamine and serotonin in our little brains increase.

We, as children, do not yet understand what is happening, but the safety and praise we receive from our parents become slightly addictive, causing us to chase after this feeling more and more. We subconsciously start seeking that affirmation in every possible way to tell ourselves that we're worthy of our parents' love. Some parents give their love freely without recourse, while others feel the need to remind their children that they are indebted to their parents for simply existing in this world. Some of us may have known the latter type of parents. Every statement of gratitude and positive gesture comes at a price for their kids. These types of parents will lend a helping hand when they know their kids need it, saving that gesture in their back pocket as a loan, which they will bring up later when an inconvenience occurs. Or they will ask their children to do a task they can easily do themselves but manipulate them into doing it by using their loving gestures as payment, thus controlling the household. The moment the kids dare to fight back or set boundaries, they are met with tactical victimization, or their parents are likely to lash out irrationally to prove they are in control.

In some cultures, words and physical affection simply cannot do justice to the required praise, so the parents don't bother giving it. A friend of mine who grew up in Tongan culture shared that while he was growing up, he did not receive much affection or appreciation for his helpfulness and devotion to his family. Instead, it was up to him to figure out the depth of love his parents had. Imagine being raised in a home where you never hear the words "I love you" from your parents or never receive a hug from them. Instead, you're only reminded that your basic needs are being met. It can get confusing, especially when you're living in a society where people have polar opposite environments in their homes and even on television. Now, this can vary based on generations, but for the sake of this book, we will focus on the first generation. In some cultures, love doesn't even exist as a sustainable concept, but meeting expectations makes you an obedient child, and obedience makes you favorable not just to your parents but to the world.

Due to this mentality, a child is reduced to the level of an animal that must be trained, but unlike animals, human brains are more complex. We feel beyond hunger, fear, rage, and joy. There's a learned emotion called guilt. So, it isn't just a matter of following rules because anyone can make or break rules, but when you add cultural guilt, the rules almost feel ironclad, and the fear of consequence outweighs any desire to pursue personal passions or attempt to separate yourself from the collective you call your family. In most immigrant cultures, similar to Lebanese culture, failure is not an option, yet modern society preaches that success comes from moments of failure.

Our parents constantly remind us of the struggles they went through to provide for us as our mothers raised us and our fathers provided all the material goods and safety we needed to survive. Speaking from the perspective of men, we were taught that a man's role in the house is to be a successful provider who does not cry when things get challenging or show emotion in general. Dads seemed to exemplify that. It's not that they were emotionless, but they had to be the stable rock our family could lean on when challenges arose. They may not have shown much emotion like our mothers, but they did show up when it counted. While learning their backstory, mixed with a little added guilt, we then place an internal expectation on ourselves to be what our parents were, because anything short of that is a failure, walking the world with a handicap unlike our white counterparts.

Similarly, immigrant women and mothers place a lot of pressure on their daughters. As I observed growing up with female cousins, they had to be intelligent, well-rounded, and must connect with peers in the culture, and they could not date outside of their culture. This is why my cousins dated their boyfriends in complete secrecy. If different ages were involved, which was the case for my two cousins, the oldest daughter would have the strictest rules placed on her while her younger sister would enjoy more leniency. I don't know what it was about the age gap that created this noticeable difference, but it was there.

My oldest female cousin, while in high school, was not allowed to attend her homecoming dance during her freshman year, while her younger sister was allowed to go without question. As her younger sister was preparing for the dance, you could sense the older sister's resentment, not having the opportunity to create the memory her sister was about to generate. Yet they both faced the same expectations: to gain a successful career, find a man—ideally from the same culture or from a "good family," so to speak—and produce grandbabies for their parents to bask in.

Parents expect great things from us, and these expectations are embedded in us from the moment we're born and continue through adulthood. In such cultures, it's common for individuals to seek affirmation and love from other places outside the home when they don't feel they are receiving any from their parents. The way we process all these positive emotions as adults is dictated by the ways and sources from which we receive these affirmations and feelings of care. By definition, this is called "Classical Conditioning." This is how children are taught to differentiate between good and bad behavior through punishment and praise. In some cases, there isn't much praise, but rather more critique. For example, a child may have a natural talent for something like music, drawing, or athleticism.

As the child tries to share these talents with their parents, they are often dismissed or critiqued in a way that makes this talent feel unimportant, imposing the view that they will not be able to succeed or lead a sustainable life. Have you ever studied for a challenging exam in school, scared that you would fail, only to be surprised when you passed with a B+? You end up receiving praise from your teacher, so you decide to share this news with your parents, only to be criticized for not getting a higher grade. It doesn't feel good, does it?

In the case of classical conditioning, some cultures condition their children unknowingly. They seem to want the best but fail to understand that compassion and positive praise can yield exponential growth and confidence in oneself. They use fear and guilt as their measures. Their continuous criticism about anything that isn't up to their standards, without understanding the perspective of their child, breaks down any confidence the child might possess. We, as children, grow up with the instilled feeling that when we cannot do anything remotely correct, no matter how small our success may be, it won't be good enough. And if we dare to do something completely opposite of our parents' desires, well… be prepared for their wrath.

In my case, this pressure and my parents' cultural value system meant that every decision my parents made was absolute because that's just how things were in our culture. To go against that is to go against the family. If you went against the family, you were a disappointment and an embarrassment. There was no discussion or dialogue: "End of discussion!" before the discussion even started. In fact, in my culture, parents predetermine our life goals before we're even conceived. In some parts of Lebanon, the parents would go as far as arranging marriages while the child was still young enough to walk. When I was 13 years old, my seventh-grade teacher informed my mother about my creative talents. She tried to persuade my mom to enroll me in an art school, as my drawing skills were years ahead of my age. My mom started laughing and confidently stated that I was going to become a doctor. I wasn't mad or anything because I did not understand the weight of what she had said. This is what most immigrant parents expect from their children: to be a doctor or lawyer, something thought to have tangible merit and yield a high income. This, alongside abrasive disciplinary punishments for any misconduct, was what you could expect on a day-to-day basis.

It makes sense to think that all of these expectations and strict rules are in place to ensure the success of a child's future, and in most cases, that would be the reality. But in other cases, such as mine, it felt more like a way for parents to flaunt their successful children in front of their peers. These expectations were a way for parents to showcase titles like MD, DDS, etc., next to their kids' names, along with the wealth that came with it. They love to boast about their ability to afford whatever they want, whenever they want. In most immigrant households, success is defined by the amount of money they possess. For our immigrant parents, money is usually the only way to acquire power, success, security, and respect, given that some immigrant families come from impoverished regions with limited access to healthcare, food, water, and even proper shelter. Choosing a career that yields high monetary value and sounds impressive to tell others means everything to these families. Anything short of that—anything their children are passionate about that doesn't make them tangibly rich—is not worth pursuing, like my passion for art.

Even though I had always been an artistic individual since childhood, I was constantly reminded that art was just a hobby for me and not something that should be taken seriously. It wouldn't have looked good to my parents' peers if they had raised a starving artist. If I had chosen art as my career, I would've lost my parents' respect; more importantly, I would've lost the title of "A Good Child." If I wanted to keep this title, I had to choose a career path that would be a reason for my parents' pride when they told their friends or my extended family about it. With constant comparisons to other children in our circle or family, my parents dialed up the pressure to succeed really fast. Now, as an adult, I see my cousins and family friends as equals, taking up careers in the medical field or other high-value jobs, and almost none of them are in the creative sector. I just want to ask, "If you didn't have the pressure of pleasing your parents, what career would you have chosen instead?"

In most immigrant families, the children are extensions of their parents through cultural principles. At least, that's what I was always taught as a kid. Our duty is to be an extension of them just because they gave birth to us. I think this lesson came into play as immigrant parents left their families in their home country and had to start a new. Once they built up their families it was now the child's duty to uphold all of the history, culture, and dignity of their parents who so valiantly came to the USA for a better life. This meant that every action, decision, and consequence directly reflected our parents and their ability to raise a child. We essentially never gained an identity outside of our family. In fact, we are our family. Their complete success and absolute failure depended on us and our ability to show the world, or the close group of people they called friends and family, that we were the reason for their pride or their embarrassment. If the parent of a child had wronged someone in any way in the past, the crimes of the parent would be inherited by the child in the adult's eyes. I'm sure you've heard your parents gossip about someone's child, saying, "He's just like his father!" Any time my mother or father would have a conversation about family, it always had the word "we" in it. It almost felt like they were afraid of our independence—a fear that if your child develops their own voice, possibly an identity outside of the family, it would mean the end of their obedient child. My twin brother and I, as their children, had to do as we were told and couldn't question their rules or decisions. We just had to silently accept the consequences of things that weren't even our fault or under our control. Sounds a bit like a dictatorship, doesn't it?

Now, I am aware that being part of a family means you have to be a team player to make everything work. You have to help your parents whenever possible and not disrespect them. But in our household, my brother and I were the team, and our parents were the referees, whose job was just to call out any violations they observed—with belts and slippers as their penalties and cutting comments about their disappointment as their whistles. Have you ever gotten a bad grade on a report card, and your parents said that you were embarrassing them? Or if you're at a family outing and, before you step foot at your destination, your parents say, "Don't embarrass me!" in an assertive tone to ensure you would be scared?

It's almost as if our existence as their children would be an inconvenience for them unless we made them look good in others' eyes. I'm not saying that, as a parent, we shouldn't try to teach our children how to behave in certain environments. If we skip these lessons, we'd have children acting out at the most inopportune times. But we have to keep in mind that children are children, and their bursts of energy or moments when they forget your lessons are inevitable. These mishaps do not reflect their parents' ability to raise or teach a child. Yet, immigrant parents will still identify themselves with their children's behavior. It's like buying a newborn puppy and expecting it to be housebroken after one or two potty lessons. If they expect this from the puppy, then obviously, every time it poops on the carpet, they'll end up thinking they're bad dog owners or that the dog is just a bad dog. Perfect children are not a thing. Yet, as soon as children are old enough to grasp the concepts of right and wrong, they are put under pressure to act exactly as their parents expect them to. This is where we understand control and power.

Unlike my American peers, whose parents allowed them to carve their own paths and make their own choices at a certain age, we were not allowed to stray away in any sense. Some of my peers were able to make big life choices as soon as they turned eighteen, such as moving away to college with the support of their parents, while more ethnic families value their cultural perimeters, and anything outside of that is considered disobedience. I was unaware of the complete ownership of my life until I reached my 30s. Everything was about family for my parents, even when it had nothing to do with family.

Every time I tried to separate myself from my family and just be Jonathan—not the son of my parents—I would immediately get sent on a guilt trip by them, especially by my mother. Guilt-tripping was one of her specialties. She would use tactics like asking me, "Why would you leave me?" in a tone that would make me feel ashamed, as if I were abandoning her in the middle of a forest to fend for herself. If that didn't work, she would use more aggressive tactics. If I ever did anything she disapproved of, or if I ever tried to stand up for beliefs of mine that were different from hers, she would immediately start saying that she no longer had a son named Jonathan. After getting some time away from her and a quick command from my dad, I had to apologize to her. She was my mother, after all. She would forgive me, and once again, I would be roped back into my family collective, with whatever identity I had gained for myself slowly fading away.

Once, I had an argument with my mother, which ultimately turned into a screaming match because I wasn't feeling heard as she asserted her dominance. After it was over, we separated, and I went into my room and angrily slammed my door. My dad intervened, as he had asked me to go and apologize to my mom, knowing she may have been wrong. I walked up to her; she didn't even make eye contact with me. I apologized for starting an argument and gave her a kiss on the cheek. She pursed her lips and said, "You really hurt my feelings," and continued with whatever chore she was doing while reminding me she was justified, not leaving the previous argument in the past. Even though my mother always got what she wanted, I still had to earn her affection. It was something that wasn't given out freely, and I was no longer her good child for having created such animosity between us instead of just following her blindly.

Remember how I said that children innately know when they misbehave and when they do something good, depending on whether they get rewarded or punished? Well, growing up, we certainly knew it when we misbehaved. I grew up in the 90s when spanking your kids was still acceptable and not frowned upon. It was my parents' favorite method of behavior modification. Although I don't fault them for how they chose to discipline us—because that was most probably the way they were disciplined growing up—to a degree, some instances felt more malicious than others. On the one hand, my mom used to tell us how much she loved us and would do anything to ensure our safety. On the other hand, my mom cornered my brother and me in the hallway to discipline us with her belt. Our house had a J-shaped hallway with two doors on each end. She had locked one of the doors and scurried us into the hallway as if we were mice trying to find a way out of a man-made maze. She proceeded to hit us with her leather belt multiple times. This was the usual form of discipline, but sometimes it just felt like the disciplining went too far.

There was a particularly memorable moment when my brother and I were ten years old. On that day, we were fooling around outside the house, as kids do, before going to school. My brother ended up getting hurt just as we were supposed to be on our way to school. My mom had to handle the situation, and we inevitably made it to school late, as usual. Later that same day, our mom took us to our aunt's house after school. We thought that it was just a routine visit to see her sister, and we got to see our cousins. As it turned out, we were wrong.

As we sat in the den, watching TV at their house, all of a sudden, I heard the front door open, and our uncle bolted in, screaming, "WHERE ARE THEY!?" He came directly into the den and dragged me into my little cousin's bedroom. He then instructed my cousin to grab the thinnest belt she could find. I was by myself and extremely confused as to what was happening. My cousin's room had two twin beds on each side of the room. They were close enough to each other that if you sat on the edge of one bed, you would be able to touch the other one at arm's length.

My uncle started screaming at me, asking me why I was giving my mother a hard time. Since I was just ten, confused, and afraid, I stayed quiet. This caused him to get more frustrated, and in his rage, he threw his hand at me and whipped the belt across my face. He then proceeded to push my face backward so that the back of my head hit the wall. At this point, I think my uncle also realized that he had taken things too far. So, he dragged me out of the room and ordered me to stand in the corner, saying, "You will stand here facing the wall with one leg in the air, and if I see your leg touch the ground, I'm gonna bring you back in and kick your ass!"

As a result of going through these sorts of punishments, I now possess exceptional core strength as an adult.

He then dragged my brother into the room. I don't know the extent to which he disciplined my brother, but I know that it wasn't nearly as horrific as what I had experienced. I remember ending this interaction in tears, screaming at my mom that I no longer considered her my mother for allowing someone to come in and hurt me that way. It felt less like discipline and more like abuse. Without a guilty conscience, she took us home.

My parents made sure that we knew when we did something wrong so that the limited affection we received from them when we behaved would mean much more. This became an everyday occurrence in our household, where classical conditioning was normal for me. I knew my place in the house, and I also knew what would set my parents off. This may sound a tad extreme, but this is what it takes to survive in an immigrant household. As a child of immigrant parents, you had to anticipate their next move before making yours. This was not just about your parents but your extended family as well. It would not be an exaggeration to say that they took the statement, "It takes a village to raise a child," a little too seriously. Every adult in our immediate family had the green light to beat the living daylights out of us if we acted up in front of them.

Things would escalate from 0 to 100 very quickly and take a while to dial back down. There was never a middle ground for emotions. I would constantly be walking on eggshells every day to avoid invoking the wrath of the powers above (my parents, aunts, uncles, and even grandparents). My life was filled with constant, unexpected chaos. The chaos that ensued in my home wasn't always necessarily negative. There were fun moments of chaos that I enjoyed, which mostly happened during family gatherings where children would run around, play games, and eat lavish dishes, and the children would not be reprimanded for acting out. This is the plus side of living in an immigrant household. The level of camaraderie and the feeling of togetherness is unmatched. I don't think I have ever witnessed an American family with this same level of camaraderie and closeness among them, but I have also not seen such an extreme level of behavioral discipline in them either. There were times when the negative chaos felt more abundant than the positive, but this is what I know.

Chapter 2: Family Dynamics

Every family has its quirks and flaws, as did mine. In many immigrant homes, boys are usually treated differently than girls; while the boys were babied, fed, and lightly reprimanded for bad behaviors, girls seemed to have it worse. They were constantly under scrutiny regarding what they wore and who they spent time with. The eldest children had stricter rules than their younger siblings, among many other contradictory guidelines. I assumed it was because in some families the eldest being their first child was the child where parents were figuring it out. The fears, the excitement, the frustrations, new parents were not always able to get it right. My situation was interesting. I grew up with a twin brother, born a minute apart. He and I were treated like completely different children,

As I delved into my past, all the puzzle pieces started to fit together. The way we were treated as children mirrored how we were as adults. We were born in 1990 in a typical three-bedroom home in the suburbs. We had a pretty typical upbringing, went to private school, and had friends in the neighborhood with whom we often spent time. My mom was a stay-at-home mother for the first ten years of our lives before going to work, while my dad worked as a CPA for a grocery store. Most nights, we ate dinner as a family, and our mom would help with our homework while Dad was working. My parents took the family on fun vacations when they could; of course, we have all the family photos to prove it. From the outside, we were a picture-perfect family. Though that was not a complete lie, there were some things that stayed behind closed doors.

In my adulthood, I found that while my brother and I both shared the womb, upon the day of our birth, my umbilical cord wrapped around my brother, which landed him in the NICU for an additional three weeks. He was a lot smaller than me, and his color was reddish-purple due to the lack of oxygen. Eventually, my parents discovered that he had to have the most expensive baby formula flown in from out of the country because his stomach wouldn't tolerate any basic formula produced in the States. Due to his unhealthy appearance, my parents took extra care of my brother, and it showed.

At the same time, I came out happy and healthy, able to breastfeed, and was, in fact, a quiet, happy baby with an independent attitude. I was a little too independent, which drove my parents crazy, as my brother would cling to my mom, my dad, or whoever carried him. I was squirming to get down on the ground to walk around and explore. This set the trajectory for how we both lived the bulk of our lives into adulthood. My brother was coddled through adulthood, whereas I was considered the more mature, stable child. So, I naturally received a lot more pressure and higher expectations. These expectations were placed in a very subtle way, often through stories and superstitions.

When I was old enough to understand, my parents told me that I used to have very bad night terrors. I would cry hysterically until my mom came in and blessed me with some holy water and said a prayer. It almost sounded like I was being possessed. The reason for this is that in our culture, we have something called "the evil eye." If you don't understand what that means, it refers to someone appreciating or coveting what you have so much that they unknowingly wish harm upon it.

My mom told me that at one point, it was so bad that she and my aunt had to come into my room and say prayers in two completely separate languages while blessing me with holy water to finally calm me down and help me fall back asleep. I asked my parents why someone would do that. They explained to me that, being Middle Eastern, you don't typically have children with fair skin and fair hair, which I did. It was a very rare form of beauty, as I understood it from my parents. My brother had a darker complexion and thick dark hair. Because of this fact and our differing personalities, my parents called me "a good son." Maybe not outwardly, but it definitely showed how proud they were that I was their kid, based on my sheer appearance and my do-gooder attitude.

My parents used a lot of superstition and religion to teach lessons to us, but it was somewhat geared toward their benefit. They scared us into making sure we did what they asked without question or behaved like model children. Though this never seemed to phase my brother, I was more fearful for some reason. I let my mom decide all of the clothes that I would wear growing up to the point where I knew what she would pick out for me before she did and would make sure to show her to gain her affection. I was very well-spoken at a young age, artistic and creative, and I would even seek my mother's opinion on most occasions when it came to things I created and outfits I wore. I knew my mom enjoyed me and always asked for my opinions. I would help her get ready for outings and go shopping with her. It felt like we were buddies. It's not like my brother and I didn't get into serious trouble growing up, but there were definitely moments when I made my mother want to rip her hair out.

We were definitely very mischievous. At one point, my mother had to call in reinforcements with my uncle to come discipline us because we were driving her crazy as I had shared in the previous chapter. She didn't know what else to do. But that didn't change the fact that I recognized the difference in parenting styles my parents used between my brother and me in the coming years. It wasn't something I was consciously aware of, but I definitely enjoyed the praise I received from my parents. Moreover, the affection that followed the praise whenever I did something good was something they would want to share with their friends—or even just to look like a model family at church or other outings where my mom would be seen by her peers, which she prided herself on.

Perfection was at the top of our priority list. We had to look perfect and act perfect to maintain the respect of my parents' peers. Wearing the nicest outfits, putting on her best jewelry, wearing her designer perfume, and ensuring that we drove the most expensive car to church rather than her everyday minivan were all part of this act. This also included mothers, including mine, sitting around in their Sunday best, bragging about the merits and awards their children received, gossiping about whose dirty laundry made it into the public eye, mixed in with half-genuine smiles and kisses on the cheek. It felt like an unspoken competition between families that really turned up the pressure.

I didn't realize that there was a clear difference between how my brother was viewed compared to myself. Not to say that my parents didn't love my brother in the same way or that they thought he was a bad child; they seemed to give him a little extra attention—a different type of attention than they gave me. It was later realized in our teen years that we were no longer children in my parents' eyes and that we were young adults who had to understand how the world worked. We were now the men of the house, next to my father, of course.

At the age of 15, I experienced one of the scariest moments of my life when I almost lost my father. He suffered from a brain aneurysm that he fortunately survived. It landed him in the ICU for weeks and then in a common hospital room for three months. But we'll get back to that story in just a minute.

During that time, my mom kept telling my brother and me that we needed to take care of her because my dad was not home and that we were now the men of the house. I needed to take up some sort of space similar to my dad, all in hopes of making my mother feel safer at home without him there. Living through this scare while I was in high school, I had to remind myself that I was the man of the house. I had to be strong for my dad and had to be a good son. I had to put 110% into everything I did, whether it was studies or my extracurricular sports. This had no direct correlation to my dad getting better; in fact, it was a pressure I felt I had to put on myself because of my mom's request to be the man of the house.

I also want to add a little tidbit my mother told me while we were growing up: "You may be a minute older than your brother, but that means years more mature mentally." Imagine that! Putting your son or child on such a high pedestal to be the more mature twin brother. But what did that mean? I didn't understand what that fully meant at the time. I was too young to get a job or drive a car. All I had experienced was going to school and playing sports while navigating the awkwardness of being 15 years old. It felt like an obligation that I had to uphold to my family, as I was the older one.

Though my brother clung to my parents and just wanted to be coddled, I was more stubborn and wanted to be on the ground walking around. We ended up growing to be very opposite teens compared to when we were children. My brother, who seemingly needed reassurance, was popular, a class clown, and very athletic, whereas I was the complete opposite—contrary to my stubborn, explorative attitude as an infant. I was chubby, went through an awkward stage, was heavily bullied, and was not considered funny at all. You could say that I was very insecure and shy about who I was, and at that time, I also had a very big secret that I didn't fully understand. I battled with this deep, dark secret that I could not tell anyone for fear that I would no longer be the perfect little son. In the back of my mind, I remembered what my mother had told me: that I had to be the man of the house and that I was more mature than my brother. I dove into my studies and my extracurricular activities, such as cross country and track and field. I even took on a part-time job throughout the remaining years of high school. This was all to prove that I could be a part of a family that could not easily be thrown out. Due to my busy schedule and my people pleaser personality my parents became more lenient with me, compared to my brother. For the most part I had free rein to come and go as I pleased using my work schedule, practice or study group excuses to my advantage. Without hesitation my parents would say "drive safe" and I would be on my way. I used this tactic to my advantage whenever my gay emotions started rearing it's head at me. I was just as intrigued as I was afraid of exploring them, nervously leaving my home knowing that I was not going to be where I told my parents.

At the age of 16, I started to explore my sexual orientation with individuals to ensure this would not be traced back to me; I would connect with people not in my friend group or within the same city limits for good measure. I had my driver's license and the trust of my parents, so getting out of the house was not as challenging as I had assumed. When I followed through with my encounters, I would leave those experiences in disgust with myself. I emotionally punish myself afterward, telling myself it was just a phase and that I would be a bad son if this became my true reality. I kept convincing myself it would not happen again because I had gotten it out of my system. I did this all while taking a scorching hot shower to wash away my "unclean deed" and vomiting in the sink, as if purging would also undo where my lips explored. This punishment came from a deep-rooted guilt that what I was doing was not acceptable to my family and cure those emotions as if they was a virus I was trying to ride out. Nobody seemed to have figured anything out because of my consistently busy school, sports, and work schedule but the fear would follow me

At this time, my brother and I attended different high schools. After his first semester at our initial high school, he received too many demerits for being a popular class clown, and the school decided not to allow him to continue learning there. So, while I was doing my thing without question, my parents were focusing their attention on my reckless twin brother. This is when I started to recognize my role in the family as “the good son.” I could remain at the private high school that my parents paid so much money for while my brother created some stress for my parents, having to relocate him to another high school nearby. Though I received this title as the good son because of my ability to be self-sufficient without causing friction at home, they still seemed to give my brother a little extra attention.

Eventually, my self-sufficiency would cause me internal stress, as receiving support from my parents when it counted was few and far between. Because of my go-getter attitude, it was assumed that I would do a good enough job in academia and sports. When I received an award or merit, it was met with a dismissive flick of their wrist while saying in a monotone voice, "Good," as if it were expected. On the other hand, if my brother wanted anything, all he had to do was scream and cry, and after a heated argument, he would get it. If I wanted anything, I was met with a "NO." I would try to follow the same tactic as my brother, but I would fail miserably, as I did not get most of the things I wanted outside of the necessities in my teen years or did not voice my requests knowing the outcome.

Here's an example: When we were both old enough to drive, I was the first of us to pass my written exam and my physical driving test and receive my license. Though my parents were working in the upper middle class, we did not have enough money to get me my own car, so my uncle and cousins gave me hand-me-downs. By the time my brother got his driver's license, I was already in my third hand-me-down car. This was over the span of almost a year. My brother was very much into having a pickup truck and begged my parents to get him a used Silverado that was lifted and pewter gold. It wasn't anything to rave about, but it was what my brother wanted. I think it was because all his school friends had some sort of pickup truck.

My parents struck a deal with my brother, saying, "If you bring us passing grades on your report card, we will get you the truck"—not a deal that I ever got when I received my license. Shortly after that deal was made, my brother threw a massive fit, fearing that the truck would be sold before his report card came out. My parents went to the car lot, purchased the truck, revised their deal, and said, "We got you the car that you wanted, so now make sure you get us the grades that we want!"

The report card came out, and my parents were more than disappointed because he had failed all his classes yet still received his prize. As unfair as this was, it was a constant recurring theme. I started to feel unseen by my parents. Though I moved in silence at home, I figured my actions would speak louder than my words, but sadly, they did not. My actions were overshadowed by my brother's temper tantrums and continuous troublemaking. I started acting out in some ways. I would often stay out on weekends with friends or sneak away for a secret rendezvous with a stranger. If they asked where I was going, I would snap in a mini rage, frustrated that they would start acting like concerned parents at that exact moment when they didn't seem excited about any successful parts of my teenage life.

Eventually, when I turned 18, I transferred everything my parents had given me into my name. It was my underhanded way of being rebellious because if my parents weren't going to be present for all my successes, then why should they have the ability to take anything away from me? Now, I was still in high school, so it wasn't much to switch over to my name, but it felt satisfying to do it alongside my dad. I had a cell phone and a couple of credit cards. I want to point out that I was, and still am, very calculated in my decisions. This was no random act of rebellion; it was what I felt was my only way to control my life in a manner that made sense since I felt I could not control my parents' attention.

I was working at my uncle's restaurant on the weekends during my senior year in high school. My uncle needed the extra help and offered to pay me under the table. I was very money-hungry and excited to be pocketing a whopping $10 per hour without taxes; the minimum wage in 2008 was around $8 per hour. The hours were intense, but I was young, and it wouldn't interfere with my schooling or sports. I wanted to make money and be helpful because that would make me more valuable to my family. Just picture my uncle praising me to my parents about my work ethic. The thought felt really nice. I was working 12-hour shifts on Saturdays and Sundays, closing and opening up the restaurant and driving back home after closing on Sunday to make it in time to sleep for my school week. I did this for the remainder of my senior year and saved up about $5,000 after bills and some enjoyment in my financial freedom.

Alongside working, I was an athlete during my four years in high school. I ran cross-country and track. However, my first couple of years were challenging. Once I reached my junior year, I wanted to become more enveloped in my sport—running on weekends and overthinking everything I ate. I even stopped participating in the weekend house parties my friends would throw to become better at my sport. I wanted to get a scholarship to college. In fact, I had to. I knew that because my plan was to become a doctor. My parents did not approve of my passion for making art full-time. I still wanted them to be proud of me. That younger version of myself longed to hear those words of affirmation. If it wasn't going to be now, maybe it would be one day. So, I set my goal in motion to become an ideal candidate for a scholarship to college. During the process of applying, we scheduled meetings with guidance counselors to help us determine the best fit based on GPA, extracurricular activities, volunteer work, and SAT scores. Though I was studious enough, I wasn't the smartest kid in school, so my GPA was pretty average. My counselor told me that the only school that would consider me was Cal State University. As long as I passed their proficiency exam, I would be admitted, but I was not a great standardized test taker. My SAT score was an embarrassment, scoring 1145 out of 2400. All of my friends in class were better exam takers than I was.

I remember a friend of mine scored 2000 points out of 2400 on the SAT, and I jokingly said, "Did she spell her name wrong?" You were also scored based on the input of your personal information. Closer to the end of the year, I received a letter from a well-known college, UC San Diego. They had personally requested that I apply, as they wanted to offer me a partial scholarship. In sheer excitement, I showed my mother the letter, thinking she would be ecstatic as I was one step closer to fulfilling her dream of becoming a doctor. However, her emotions did not mirror mine. She immediately dismissed me, saying I was too young to move away from home and could go to our local community college instead. I was devastated, to say the least. The thing I thought would impress my mom didn't. I felt I had no control over the outcome of my life, even when I set aside my passion to pursue the career path my parents expected from me. I was convinced I couldn't win.

After feeling unseen by my parents and my guidance counselor, I took action to increase my level of independence and made what I considered a lot of money at the time. I was desperate to be recognized as a valuable part of my family and society. I decided to expand my independence further and start planning my move out of my parents' home with a couple of friends from school. I was creating my own habits in how I lived, feeling unable to thrive in my parents' home. I had a rich history of being Lebanese, but my present and future lessons were being taught in an American environment. It was as if I was battling two opposing identities. My friends and I sat down together and started talking about budgets and where we would live. We also began the hunt for an apartment. Being the product of immigrant parents, I knew they would not be keen on letting their 18-year-old son move out. In most immigrant households, kids tend to stay living in their parent's home through adulthood.

The way it was presented to me was that it was viewed as family abandonment. My parents would reference how they were not like American parents. They don't "throw" their kids out at eighteen, as if American parents are barbarians who only nurture their kids until they reach legal age, then expect them to fend for themselves at whatever stage they may be in their lives. It wasn't just about American parents; they seemed to suggest that Lebanese people were the highest form of nurturers, incomparable to any other group. To rewind a bit, the cycle I witnessed growing up was that immigrant parents had their children, who grew up with them, got married, lived in the same home, and had their children in the same house where the parents became grandparents.

I slowly started to feel more and more out of place in my home. Not only did I often disagree with my parents about how I operated versus their way of operating, but I also had a big secret I was carrying close. I was afraid I would make a misstep, and everyone would find out before I was ready or if I even wanted to come out at all. I lived in fear for a couple of months leading up to my graduation. My plan was that after graduating, I would get an apartment and become the person I promised myself I would be. So, I told my parents in a flustered state. My dad said that if I could afford rent, then I could afford to pay for the car I was driving, which he had initially leased for himself.

It was a 2007 Jeep Wrangler Unlimited that I was driving during my last year of school. My dad had gotten the car for himself but quickly realized he wasn't enjoying it, as it was not comfortable for his longer commute to work. So, he decided to let me drive it to school for the duration of the lease term. I, too, became frustrated because I knew I could not afford rent and all my other expenses, including a $450 monthly car payment. Once I heard this, he gave me an ultimatum: either I give him the keys to the Jeep and move out, or I stay home and continue driving the car. Being the stubborn man that I am, I handed him the keys, remembering that he had purchased a car from an auction a month earlier, and it was sitting in the backyard untouched.

I said, "I will take the car in the back since it's paid off, and I won't need to make payments." My dad was so floored that I called his bluff. A couple of months later, after I continued driving this used car and was happy with my decision, my dad came to me later on and begged me not to move out. He was bribing me with an offer to get one of five cars he had selected if I didn't move out.

At this time, he was not aware that my plans to move out had fallen through because all three of my soon-to-be roommates did not have a credit score. I was the only one working since I was sixteen, so I had a credit score and was not comfortable putting my credit on the line. I decided to take up the offer from my dad. I thought back to when my dad bought my brother that Silverado and felt vindicated. We traded in the rust bucket I was driving, and I chose a 2009 Mitsubishi Lancer in bright metallic red. As the summer continued, I enjoyed my car until my dad came up to me after helping me get it. He handed me an envelope with a smirk and said, "Here is your car payment." Looking at him, I replied, "What do you mean?" He then stated that he was only willing to help me get the car, not pay for it.

That feeling of vindication immediately left my mind, and my heart sank into my stomach. This man who had begged me to stay home a couple of months earlier, with the bribe of giving me something I was content on not having out of principle, had lied to me once I gave in. I was now responsible for another monthly expense I was unprepared to take on and had been talked back into the toxic household I was desperately trying to leave. My savings account quickly dwindled as the expenses of a new car developed. Unlike my brother, I did not receive much assistance from my parents; in fact, I received more requests for favors from them. I obliged, feeling obligated to relieve them of the burden of having two reckless, unreliable children. I felt it was my duty to maintain the status of being a good son. After all, my dad did get me a new car. I blew through my savings, leaving me poorer than I was at 18 years old, fresh out of high school. Desperate not to be bothered by my parents to complete tasks they could easily do themselves, I spent most of my summer out of the house, working at my uncle's restaurant in Long Beach or hanging out with my friends until the school year started. Though I was a good son, my brother was still the favorite, as he needed constant attention and aid from my parents.

As soon as my term in junior college started, I remained busy. Going into junior college was vastly different than I had expected. To be a full-time student, you needed to have

15 credits or 3-4 classes every quarter. To avoid the toxic environment at home, I made sure to space out my classes so I would be on campus all day. Some days, I would be on campus so late that my parents would call me frantic about why I was not home. I had this goal in mind: if I could be successful enough, I could get a great job, move out of my parents' house, and live the authentic life I saw fit. That was far from what happened. I was a struggling college student like any other teenager.

I worked a part-time job that paid very little, wanted to remain social and have that "college experience," and tried to pass all my classes. However, my ability to be more studious in college than in high school fell short. I was a very average-scoring college student, paying my hard-earned money to struggle in these classes. How is it that college is so expensive, costing about $300-400 per class, and if I was late to a chem lab, I was not allowed to participate, resulting in an absence on my record? I was essentially paying for punishment. The campus that would have been my home away from home was starting to cause me stress.

I was barely passing my classes. I wasn't making enough money to afford my classes on top of my other expenses and my brother's occasional requests for money. I did not want to be at home for fear that my parents would need more from me. I was just trying to survive. I left my job at my uncle's restaurant since the commute with school became too much, and I found something at a local retail store in the mall. At this time, my brother had his first job at Subway. Given my brother's history, he never seemed to be able to save his paycheck. It could have been him trying to impress his girlfriend, whom I graduated high school with, or he was unnecessarily buying things. However, I was straying away from home. My parents still viewed me as the good son, as I was in school, working, and being as independent as I could be. My brother was very cryptic about the classes he was enrolled in at another local community college. He was always broke, asking my parents for money and throwing a tantrum anytime they implemented any rules. Yet I felt compelled to overshare with my parents just for them to use it against me in the future while I was seeking separation from them. Crazy, I know.

Eventually, my parents could not deal with my brother's antics, so they asked me to step up and help him. Little did I know I was walking into a trap. I became an extension of my parents, doing the dirty work they had no bandwidth for. In essence, I became a parent to my brother.

Now, it is common for most families to have older siblings look out for their younger counterparts. Why shouldn't they? They have been in this world longer; they should know the rules, and it makes teaching the younger ones a lot easier. Immigrant parents take it a little further, indoctrinating the expectation that the older sibling is a direct extension of the parents and must act as such in their absence. Expecting the older child to parent the younger child is known as parentification. Parentification occurs when parents look to their children to provide emotional or practical support, causing the child to become the caregiver. This forces a child who is not emotionally or mentally ready to take on the roles and responsibilities of a parent (Staff, 2023).

Initially, I was not angry about taking on more responsibility; in fact, I really enjoyed it. It made me feel superior to my brother and garnered the respect of my parents. It almost felt like it was giving me a superpower that I didn't think I could have. Quickly, I learned that this superpower came at a price—quite literally.

At that time, my brother and I were both 19 years old, and my brother saw that I was very independent. I was able to get my own cell phone line with my own cell phone bill and purchase any cell phone I wanted. He wanted to get in on that action. He asked me if he could be on my phone plan and if I could help him get his own cell phone. I said "OK," with the understanding that we would alternate paying the phone bill every month. One month, I would be responsible for the phone bill; the following month, he would be responsible, and so on.

After the first few months, I realized he had not helped at all with the cell phone bill. I distinctly remember one time looking at our phone bill, receiving a past-due notice, and, being the more responsible brother, I kept track of all the bills. My brother stated that he did not have any money to pay the $200 Verizon cell phone bill. Because of the past-due notice, the two cell phone lines cost $400. I had to pay the amount, or our phones would be disconnected or sent to collections. I found myself scolding my brother as if I were his parent and started to feel the same frustration my parents had felt with him years earlier. This was not the first time my brother had taken advantage of my generosity. There was an instance when my cousins and I decided to go bowling. We chose a specific day, which was dollar bowling night every Wednesday at our local bowling alley, and we wanted to establish a routine that our family could continue for as long as possible. My brother walked into family bowling night with a group of friends, which nobody expected, and as they geared up to bowl with our family, my brother volunteered me to pay for his group of friends. I was extremely offended. Not only was I not close to any of his friends, but my brother automatically assumed I would care for him as if I were his parent.

Furiously, I grabbed my debit card and swiped the $68 tab to pay for his friends to bowl, making him aware that I would not be covering any of the food or beverages they might want while hanging out with us. We had one of my younger cousins with us who eventually needed a ride home, and wanting to stay and enjoy my time, I asked my brother to drive my car and drop him off. Later, I found out that he was recklessly driving well above the speed limit, as my car was technically considered a street racing car.

Again, that superpower I thought I had gained by being responsible for my younger twin brother didn't feel like a superpower at all. It slowly started to feel like I was being chained down to a concrete platform, where the chain just kept getting tighter and tighter, and my body slowly went from a standing position to a kneeling position—kind of like that one scene from Blade where Ryan Reynolds is chained and held captive by vampires, minus the sweaty six-pack. Eventually, I felt I would be crushed to the ground by the weight of this responsibility. I pleaded with my parents about how I just could not sustain paying for my brother and myself, but I don't think anything came of that conversation.

In fact, this situation has occurred in various forms so many times throughout my life that they all seem to blur together. Though I was extremely frustrated and wanted to stop helping my brother, my sense of responsibility remained intact. My parents were so detached from my brother that they were not paying attention to the fact that he was skipping college classes. My brother is not the best liar; he gets his stories mixed up so often that if you keep him talking, you will catch him in a lie.

I found out my brother was skipping college and was not planning to continue attending community college after the semester ended. You're probably wondering how I caught him in the lie. He had told me he was on his way to class on a Tuesday, and I didn't think anything of it. I went about my week as usual. The following week, he should have been in class on the same day at the same time. I asked him, "Why aren't you going to class today?" It didn't take much for me to get him to admit that he was no longer going to class but was studying to join the military. He begged me not to tell my parents, and I respected his request. However, as a parent-child, I wanted to know why he felt the military would be a good fit for him. He gave me a long, drawn-out story about wanting to grow and needing discipline.

He claimed the military could provide that, and he would be going into the military with his really good friend, whom I also knew. So, while I kept the secret, my brother was studying for the standardized military exam that would place him in a branch. If you're unfamiliar with this type of standardized testing, the highest-scoring branch is the Air Force, and that was what my brother was aiming for because his friend would be entering the Air Force with him.

Unfortunately, my brother was not the greatest test taker, so it took him a few tries to get a high enough score that landed him in the Navy, while our mutual friend successfully scored in the Air Force. I let him know that he would eventually have to tell our parents he was leaving because he would be gone to Boot Camp for quite some time. He finally worked up the courage ten days before he flew away to Boot Camp and told my parents he had joined the military. Upon receiving this information, my parents were the most distraught and scared they had ever been. It scared them beyond any abrasive experience my brother could have given them. I sat back and watched the fire burn.

I knew that this would solidify my relationship with my parents as the ultimate son. I was the one who did not run away from the family. I stayed in school and worked my job, and that's all they ever wanted for their kids. I was excited to be the center of attention for my parents. I even thought I could get away with a little more and that living at home would be much easier. I would not have to parent my brother anymore, and I would remain in the good graces of my parents.

I started asking them for a little extra cash every so often, and eventually I got too ahead of myself because my parents started to catch on. My parents were a lot shrewder that I gave them credit for. We all know that sometimes parents don't always communicate with one another, so when I would ask one parent for some money and succeeded, I would sneakily go to my other parent and ask for the same amount doubling what I was hoping to get. I would ask for $20 here and there to go grab lunch with friends or money so I wouldn't have to spend all of mine of necessities like gas for my car or to make minimum payments to my credit card. It worked for a time, but they caught on. They berated me as they used to with my brother when he was home. It's not that I needed the cash desperately. I wanted to see how much I could get away with since my brother was no longer consuming their minds and in their wallets. I learned that I would not have it as easy as I thought I would which I was alright with as long as my secret never made it to the surface. The thing to note is that the act of me trying to get as much out of my parents while my brother was away, was not a matter of finances. It was my way of giving them a distraction from what I did not want them to notice about me, my dark secret. Though I was content in how my parents and I were getting on, I knew my secret would eventually have to surface.

Chapter 3: Gay Son vs. Good Son

Part I

Growing up in a very strong, masculine environment, I knew that men and women had their own set of rules in the family. Men were the strong ones who did not show any emotion that could be considered feminine. According to them, men were the ones who went outside and got their hands dirty, either working in the yard or tinkering with tools. I was more creative, spending my days inside, where I would draw and paint. I knew that I was very different from the other boys in my family. While they were roughhousing and wrestling in the house, I was with my girl cousins, playing with their Barbies. Yes, I would go outside and occasionally play sports like catch with a baseball, but that ended quickly when I threw a baseball right through my aunt's window. I decided to stick to less breakable hobbies. But something deep down inside me knew that there was something different about me, although I was too young to articulate that feeling.

When I was a little older, my oldest cousin was in high school, and she joined the cross-country team. My uncle, with whom I spent a lot of my free time when I was with my cousins, decided it would be a great idea to take all of the kids and have them exercise with our older cousin, as he was our coach and we were his little team. I remember being excited at the beginning, but that excitement quickly turned into discomfort and pain, as I was not athletic and not conditioned. I remember telling my uncle that I just couldn't do it anymore and that I was really tired. It was quite literally like a scene from one of those high school sports-focused movies where the coach screams at their athletes to be better. He proceeded to do the same. But it wasn't just him telling me that I was lazy or slacking; it was a little more pointed. He had decided to use the word "fag" in his scolding.

He screamed at the top of his lungs while we were at the base of a hill, and I was pleading to stop and go home, "Don't be a fag. We don't have any fags in this family." I already knew what that word meant. I didn't think he was calling me out on anything; that was just how he spoke. According to him, men were supposed to be strong and masculine and face any challenge without question, which I refused to do when it became too unbearable. So, I ran home and cried to my mom that my uncle was calling me names and hurting my feelings; after all, I assumed spending time with my uncle and cousins would be more fun than that. My mom just brushed it off. She said that was just the way he was and how he spoke. Later, I learned that this was an excuse, among others, that she had given her little brother.

As I got older, I became more and more curious about my sexual orientation, though I did not know the phrase "sexual orientation." It was a feeling, given that I was born in the 90s. I did not have the exposure that most teenagers have in today's world. We could access the internet using dial-up, which would tie up the phone line whenever you needed a picture painted. While I was online, curiously scrolling through different search bars about what gay men were, I stumbled upon a few links that immediately made me recognize that I liked what I was seeing, but would quickly delete the search history and log off in fear someone would catch me. I would find myself walking into the local news stand near mall and seeing the "over 18 years old "section. Though I was underage, I would still try to walk past the section a couple time see the magazine with tan, muscular men on them. I also recognize now that when I would go to the mall I would walk past the men's underwear section pretending I was looking for underwear by intensely inspecting packages but only focusing on the images the packages had. I would catch myself standing there a little too long and put them down and walk away as if they did not have what I needed.

At 12 years old, I remember looking at the computer screen in the bedroom I shared with my brother and tiptoeing from the door, making sure he would not walk in on me looking at that material online. As I feared, my brother walked in on me while I was on the Internet. I rotated my chair to see him at the door, and he ran out. While chasing him down, I tried to cover up what he saw with a lie. I immediately deleted the browser history, shut off the computer, and told him it was all a mistake. Later that week, my mother came into my room and sat me down. She had never done this before, so I knew something was up. She told me my brother had seen me on the computer looking at two men making love. She proceeded to tell me that we did not have any "gay people" in our family. That conversation immediately made me afraid of who I was or could be. I didn't know if it was a decision I would have to make or who I really was deep down.

I know I was in high school, and it seemed vastly different from my elementary or junior high life. The classes were longer. We didn't have six blocks for learning each day as we did in elementary school, and we finished school at 2 PM, which I was also not used to, having left school at 3:15 for most of my life. While I had just started high school, my oldest cousin had started college, and we all know what that means—college parties. My uncle, the same one who ran us up and down that hill, hosted the best college parties and convinced our parents to let all of the kids come over and join in all the fun. Or at least that's what I was hoping it would be. During one of these parties, which were held almost every weekend of the summer, my uncle was bragging about all of the different types of liquor that he owned. I thought it was cool because my uncle was letting me drink when I was underage, while our parents made it clear it was taboo for us, as underage kids, to touch alcohol aside from a sip given by them. He had made the statement that if I ever wanted to drink alcohol, I should make sure to do it in front of him so he could ensure that I was safe.

As the night progressed, I didn't understand how toxic the environment was about to become until I became an adult. As the shots kept getting poured and the beer cans kept opening, we minors were surrounded by college kids, both male and female. My uncle was egging all of the younger boys—me, my brother, and my younger cousin, who was twelve at the time—to pursue an older woman for the night. His joking demeanor quickly faded into frustrated anger as each of us told him we had failed at the task. At the same time, I found myself attracted to some of my male counterparts at this party. With the loss of my inhibition, I tried my hardest not to act on my desire. The sight of a conventionally attractive straight college male ripping off his shirt after a few extra drinks would make any boy struggling with his sexuality a little nervous.

In the following years, I kept things to myself, but eventually, I wanted to experience what I felt firsthand. I now felt like I was battling three different identities in one home. There was my Lebanese identity, rich in culture yet toxic in some of its social views. There was my American environment, where I was trying to assimilate with my peers at school, and then there was my gay identity that nobody but I knew. Every day, I was walking on eggshells, making sure not to say the wrong thing or act hyper-feminine. I made sure to dress the right way so people wouldn't know that I was gay. I even started dating girls at fourteen, thinking that would help convert me into a "normal boy." Looking back at how my uncle yelled at me during our exercise sessions, I could only imagine how he would treat me if he found out that I liked the same gender. I was already disappointed that I was not manly enough for my family, but I didn't want to add another level of disappointment by robbing my family of the son they had hoped for. So, I continued my experiment of dating girls, hoping that I would lose the urge to be with another male.

As soon as I got into high school, I immediately tried to find myself on my very first homecoming date. I kept my desires hidden, deflecting any comments or actions that could make anyone question my sexuality. So, I proceeded with my life in high school, focusing more on trying to become the person I needed to be, passing all my classes, and trying to make friends, which was already a challenge. It wasn't until I turned 16 years old and received my driver's license that I decided to take matters into my own hands and explore the feelings I had deep down inside, but in secret, of course.

Here's the thing: in high school, I was not conventionally attractive. To paint a better picture of what I looked like, I was 5 feet 6 inches tall, with a very round-shaped head, a prominent ethnic nose that did not fit my face, and a high-pitched voice. I was neither athletic nor muscular, though I desperately wanted to appear that way. Needless to say, I definitely wasn't popular among any of the girls in my class, nor did I have many male friends. I wanted to keep my secret where it counted, so I knew I would have to take drastic measures.

One time, while my brother was dating a classmate of mine who went to a different school, his girlfriend was a cheerleader and friends with one of the popular girls at school. My uncle was known for appreciating the beauty in women, regardless of their age, and he kept making comments about her looks openly. As we hung out at my uncle's house, prepping for a movie, he pulled me aside and told me to pursue the popular girl in class. Knowing that there was no way she would just agree to go out with me if I asked her, I devised a plan to get my uncle off my back, as this was not the first time he'd pressured me to pursue women in what felt like a forceful way.

That night, I sat my brother, his girlfriend, and her friend down in the bedroom and told my classmate I would pay her to act like she was going on a date with me to help me get my uncle off my back. I set boundaries for the night to make her feel more comfortable and offered her $20 just to be my date for the evening. We all proceeded to go to the movie, which was the most boring film I think I've ever watched. I fell asleep during the movie and was shaken awake by my date when the credits rolled.

On the car ride home, we all sat next to our respective dates—my arm wrapped around her shoulder, while my brother cuddled up next to his girlfriend. When we got back to the house, my uncle pulled me aside and proceeded to yell at me as if he had been watching me in the rearview mirror. He noticed I hadn't made any physical moves on my date during the entire car ride back. I wasn't sure whether to feel violated or concerned that I was being watched. After he yelled at me, I felt overwhelmed with frustration and the need to be heard. I snapped and yelled back, letting him know that I had paid my classmate to go on a date with me so he would leave me alone. After making my statement, I ran downstairs and hid in a corner, feeling angry and sad about the entire situation. He went into the room with my brother and the girls to confirm what I had done. We never spoke about this incident again.

After that incident, I secretly joined a gay dating site, lying about my age since you had to be 18 to create a profile. To put this website into context—which might date me—it was very similar to MySpace, the famous social network at the dawn of the Internet, but specifically for gay men. You could chat, video chat if you had a webcam, and even customize your profile page with all your likes, dislikes, and physical stats, as well as change the backgrounds and color schemes. I was desperate to explore feelings I had experienced for many years. I was afraid, being new to this experience and lying about my age, that I would often meet someone much older, likely a couple of cities away. I would concoct lies to my parents so I could leave the house for extended periods after 8 PM. Other times, I stayed up until about 2 AM, knowing everyone was asleep, and snuck out to meet someone around the corner from my house. I explored my emotions and gave in to my desires, but I always left each experience feeling disgusted with myself. In the back of my mind, everything my mom told me and how my uncle treated me surfaced, reminding me that what I was doing could get me in trouble—not to mention the embarrassment I would face if anyone ever found out.

I took scorching hot showers, scrubbing my skin clean of the "dirty deed" I had done earlier that night. I would force myself to throw up while brushing my teeth, hoping it would reverse any actions I had already committed. I told myself it was just a phase, that I wouldn't do it again, and that I just needed to explore this once. But that was far from the truth. This routine lasted throughout high school, where I would give in to my desires and then punish myself for having committed such heinous actions. I hoped I wouldn't do it again, only to find those feelings and desires strengthened over the course of a few weeks. It was an unhealthy cycle, though I was unaware of it. I just thought this was how anyone in my position would normally act. I started becoming a little lazier about hiding myself and began communicating with individuals on my personal cell phone.

Back then, texting was still fairly new, and not many phones could share photos. So, I had to do that through email, if that tidbit about MySpace hasn't dated me enough already. I remembered an instance in high school when I had just gotten the new T-Mobile Sidekick LS in chocolate brown. It was the sleekest flip phone of its time, with a keyboard, and my friends were enamored by the shiny new toy I had in my pocket. I remember giving my phone to a friend, not thinking anything of it. Less than a minute went by before she gasped as she went into my email and saw some nude photos I had sent to someone, which were never meant to see the light of day. I had never felt a deeper sinking feeling than that moment. Chills rushed up my spine, and a sensation of cold washed over my skin. My heart sank into my stomach. Was this the moment they would all find out? The thought kept me restless for a long time. My friends were very close to my brother, given that he had been at our school for a full semester and was on the cross-country team with me, but he still kept in contact with all my peers. So, naturally, I was afraid someone would spill the beans to my brother, and it would somehow get back to my parents, ruining my life.

Luckily, none of that happened, and no one ever brought it up again. As my final year of high school was coming to an end, I had an epiphany: I was truly gay, and this was no mistake. I wanted to pursue a romantic partnership with another male. But the big problem was how I would go about this. Should I continue to do this in secret? Should I slowly start telling people who were closest to me in hopes that they would be supportive? All I knew was that I wanted to be with a man. So, as soon as I graduated high school, I embarked on a personal journey to see if I could make this work for myself. I met a few people here and there in the early stages of my college career, but nothing ever really stuck until one day in oceanography class when I sat next to someone who set the trajectory for my dating life.

Here's the thing: I was still in the closet, but I was a little surer of myself and seemed to walk through the world more confidently—though nobody knew my secret. I remember sitting next to this young man who was several years older than me, as I was 19. We had the same college class, and we somehow sat relatively close together, either with him in front of me or with me in front of him. There was one lecture in which our teacher made a joke, and this handsome classmate looked back at me, seemingly checking to see if I was amused. With my newfound confidence, I made an attempt to connect with him. We hit it off immediately. We chatted here and there in class until one evening he invited me to his studio apartment. I wasn’t of drinking age, so I couldn’t provide any drinks for the hangout, leaving that all up to him while I provided mixers.

We sat in his apartment watching TV, drinking vanilla-flavored vodka mixed with orange juice because, at the time, I was obsessed with making fun mixed drinks for my college friends and me at parties. As the alcohol flowed, the tension decreased, and before I knew it, we ended up in a tickle war. Slowly but surely, our bodies drew closer together until our faces met, and our lips touched. Neither of us shied away, and we proceeded to kiss. At that moment, it was the most passionate kiss I’d ever experienced with another man. It felt safe, free of judgment, and strangely familiar.

I wasn't aware until he told me that I was the first guy he’d explored his feelings with, and I thought that was very sweet. On the other hand, I had quite an impressive body count since I was sixteen. We continued to see each other often outside of the classroom, but he made it clear that he preferred to hang out in the comfort of his own apartment. I was smitten by this experience and told myself I wanted to be in a relationship. I decided I was fully invested and didn’t question anything. We both were.

There were times when I would visit him at his restaurant for lunch, making sure to sit in his section so we could spend as much time together as possible. At the time, he was a struggling musician trying to make it in the music industry. We finally worked up the courage to have complete penetrative sex. I had no idea how that would impact our relationship, especially considering I was the very first male he had ever been with sexually.

Afterward, he told me he had written a song about the experience, which he titled "The Good Pain." I remember going to a backyard concert where he was playing with his bandmate, and he sang that song. I was completely floored, as he didn't want anyone to know we were together, yet he was singing a very emotional song that described his first sexual experience with me. Unfortunately, the excitement of something new faded quickly. Shortly after that, I started to feel flustered because I wanted to go out in public and enjoy his company, doing what regular couples do. But he wasn't ready for that.

After an argument about it, our relationship ended after six weeks. We still had a class together, and although we weren't together anymore, we managed to remain friendly. After meeting him and feeling distraught that someone I had invested emotionally in didn't work out, I talked about it with my gay manager, who was open about his orientation. Seeing how sad and frustrated I was about the situation, he invited me to a house party where I would meet the man who would become my boyfriend for the next two and a half years.

Part II

I walked into my friend's party with no expectations aside from having fun with friends. He poured me a drink in the kitchen, and I proceeded to mingle with his friends. Among his group was a gentleman who seemed to be a little more interested in me than the rest.

His name was Drew. I remember walking into the kitchen to grab another beverage and noticing that he was sitting in the living room alone. I confidently walked into the living room, sat next to him on the couch, and asked him what he was doing there by himself when the party was outside. Very cliché, I know, but we sat and chatted for about 10 to 15 minutes until he leaned over and kissed me. I wasn't sure if it was the alcohol or if he was genuinely interested, given the significant age gap—he was five years older than I was. Five years may not sound like a lot as we get older, but I was only 19 at the time, and he was 24, about to turn 25.

After that party, we exchanged numbers and texted each other over the following days, planning our very first date. I was excited yet frightened as I started to really like who this person presented himself to be. I was fed up with lying to my parents about where I would be staying or if I was going out with friends when I was really going out with another gay male. So, after speaking with this new romantic interest for a couple of weeks, I made the executive decision to tell my parents and loved ones that I was gay.

I decided to do this strategically, starting with individuals I was not super close to but had some rapport with. After I told my friends, they all showed support, met me with big hugs, and told me how proud they were of me for sharing something so significant. I then proceeded to tell my cousins, each of whom found out when I asked to spend some time with them individually. I was met with open arms and open hearts. As I started to tell more family members, I asked them not to share this information with my parents, as I planned to come out to them when the time was right.

Ironically, the family member who had yelled profanities at me growing up as a show of being the alpha male turned out to be my biggest supporter when I told him I was gay. I was prepared for a battle. I asked my uncle and his wife to lunch and had them sit across from me at the table. As I fearfully began to share one of my biggest secrets, the man I thought would flip tables and curse at me told me he would always be there to protect me. That interaction, which had been so frightening, helped build my confidence for telling my parents.

At that time, I devised a plan to take my mother out for a hike with our close family friend, who was like an aunt to me. We started our walk as she prepared my mom for the news. I then shared my secret in a soft, shaky voice, still nervous and afraid of what she might think of me.

As soon as I finished my sentence, in a fit of rage, she struck her water bottle on the floor and demanded to go back home. Once we got home, my mom started interrogating me as if I had committed a crime. She immediately asked who knew about this. I explained that she was the last person to find out, as I had already told my close family and friends, and her frustration grew. She shamed me for telling everyone before her, insisting that she wanted to "fix" me before anyone else found out. She was worried about how it would make her look to have a gay son. None of the women in her friend group or church would want to associate with her, and my decision had basically ruined her life. My coming out was hijacked by my mother's fear of rejection from her peers. She proceeded to tell me she would inform my dad, and in a shamed manner, I left the conversation, losing all the confidence I had gained from the previous positive coming-out experiences. I did not interact with my dad after that meeting for a couple of months and didn't bring anything up, as I could sense a shift in his attitude.

Shortly after the news broke, my mom was laid off from her ten-year job as a pharmacy technician at a big chain pharmacy. As she was grieving the loss of her beloved job, I asked her what had happened. She responded that it was my fault she had consumed her brain with my news, leading to an error at work, which got her fired. I then decided it was time for me to properly connect with my dad about this. I was met with the most heartbreaking response a son could hear from a parent. He told me he wished he had died during his brain aneurysm so he would never have to find out his son was gay. You can only imagine how I felt after hearing those words.

Over the following weeks, my parents had many questions, and we were all afraid. As any parent would, they needed answers to the question "Why?" They wondered if something traumatic had happened to me that caused this decision. I reassured them that I was not traumatized by anyone, physically or sexually. This was just something I had come to realize was my true identity. My mother, being the more vocal parent in this scenario, asked as many questions as she could and then theorized that it was because I had a twin brother and perhaps he received some extra genes that I was missing. She proceeded to ask me to get some blood work done. She also wanted me to see a therapist, and I would later find out that the therapist was trying to instill fear in me, telling me that I would not feel safe in a gay relationship due to all the promiscuity. It seemed that this therapist was a conversion therapist who did not have my best interests at heart, nor was I trying to mend the fractured relationship I had with my parents because of the news I had shared. I did not feel like I was my parents' good son anymore. I became the embarrassment of the family, the secret that should never have been spoken, the son who needed to be "fixed."

At this time, I started dating Drew. He came to pick me up from my parents' house, where I was living at the time. Before we left for our date, my parents asked if they could meet him. Awkwardly, he came in knowing the situation. The interrogation only lasted about five minutes but felt like a lifetime. After the date, I returned home safe and sound, and as I walked in, my parents sat me down and told me how unimpressed they were with the person I had just finished dating.

As young as I was, I was very wrapped up in emotion toward this person, and I brushed off my mom's statement. Every morning, I would walk out of my room to see my mom sitting on the couch upstairs, glancing outside the window, looking sad and distraught. I wasn't sure if it was because she had been laid off from her beloved career or because her son was gay.

Every time I left the house in the months that followed, I made sure to tell my parents how much I loved them, and every time, I would wait to hear it back but was met with a lack of eye contact and silence. Over the coming weeks, I slowly started pulling away from my parents and staying at Drew's house. Although I had only known Drew for about three weeks at that time, his home began to feel more comfortable than the one I had lived in with my parents for years.

At this point, Drew and I had been dating for about four weeks. He was still trying to impress me, so when San Diego Pride was happening, he booked us a hotel room to spend the weekend there. I was excited—no one had ever spent money on me to go to a hotel because they liked me. Being part of the gay world, I was extremely nervous yet very excited; he would be my guide. The hotel was beautiful, and the weekend started off great. We planned to go to dinner as soon as we arrived, and I was still too young to drink.

He made sure to take me to a bar that allowed underage individuals in. I think it was before 11 PM when they permitted anyone under the age of 21 to enter. They also gave you a wristband so the bartenders wouldn't serve you alcohol. That didn't bother me at all because it was my very first time at a gay bar. The following day, we went to the festival, which was the highlight of the trip. He even showed me how to sneak alcohol into a water bottle so I could participate in all the festivities with everyone else who was older than me.

As the day went on, everyone seemed to get a little drunker, except for me. After we left our last bar for the day, I was asked to drive Drew's friend's car back to their apartment, where we would hang out for the remainder of the evening. I need to make this point to help you understand how I was feeling in that apartment: I tend to get extremely nervous in a crowd of people I don't know, especially in confined quarters like someone's home. As we sat on the couch, pouring ourselves cocktails, listening to music, and laughing, a mysterious bag filled with white powder began making its way around the room. I was not oblivious to the fact that it was drugs, but I'd never seen drugs up close in person.

At this point, I'd only seen what drugs look like on TV shows and in movies, but nothing that I could tangibly hold. I was already uncomfortable, and the drugs added to the equation only made me more uneasy. As the bag made its way to Drew, who was sitting next to me, it seemed pretty empty, with just a few remnants left and powdery residue coating the sides of the bag. Without hesitation, Drew took the bag to his mouth and licked up all of the residue. Already feeling extremely out of place, I quietly got up to make myself a new cocktail. When Drew noticed something was wrong, he followed me into the kitchen and asked what was going on since there was a shift in my demeanor. I told him that I was extremely offended that he didn't even ask if it would make me uncomfortable for the person I was dating to do drugs, as he had never disclosed to me that he participated in such activity prior to the event. I could see his eyes widen and his concerned demeanor shift into rage. In a defensive manner, he made it clear that it was my fault for feeling this way and that I had no business asking him to check in with me about his drug use. I was beside myself and unsure of what to do.

I just remained quiet and went outside to make a phone call to a friend who helped calm me down. Was this the very first fight? No one could tell.

As the night went on, everybody started to slowly leave the apartment while those who remained, including me and Drew, planned to spend the night, as there was no way for us to get back to our hotel room at that time. It was now 11 PM, and since everybody had been drinking since early morning, everyone was asleep but me. I looked at Drew sleeping on the couch with his head on the armrest and drool dripping from his mouth. Was this worth it? I didn't know what to do. I called my friend, who had also been in San Diego for the weekend, and after 20 minutes of explaining the situation, she offered to come pick me up. I didn't want what my parents said a while back to be right. As much as I wanted to go, I did not have access to the hotel room where we were staying. So I told her I would be fine and that I would just stay where I was for the night since we were leaving the next morning.

The next morning rolled around, and we packed our bags from our hotel room, got into his Toyota Forerunner, and drove back from San Diego to Los Angeles. During the car ride home, I was extremely silent, and he knew why. He put his hand on my lap, apologized for how he acted toward me, and said that he would never do it again. Sad and distraught, lost and confused, I didn't know where to turn. I had no friends within the gay community as I was very new. I didn't have any other outlet but Drew. After that trip, he was on his best behavior. We went to lunch one afternoon, and during one of my rants about my parents and their lack of empathy toward me, he sternly stated that he wanted me to stop talking about the situation. He seemed to be more annoyed and frustrated with my coming out than wanting to be supportive. It definitely felt like a familiar environment to my parents. Still, I ignored it because I was receiving some form of affection and love from this person when I was not receiving it from my parents. Notice any similarities?

Over the following months, I grew more attached, yet he didn't seem as attached to me in the same way. Being still underage, he was off at the gay bars of West Hollywood with his friends while I waited for the next time I would get to see him. In my naive state, I was unaware of the toxic relationship I would be in for the following couple of years.

I found myself wanting to receive the approval of this person in place of my parents. I wanted to spend time with him while he would loudly vocalize that he needed time for himself, meaning he wanted to go out drinking with his friends. He started to make me feel as if I was not on his level due to our age gap, which stung, but I let him get away with it because I didn't feel safe and happy at home. The love I was so desperately seeking from my parents at that time was absent.

After five months of dating, he ended things with me. He said he was not over his previous relationship, which I had gathered after I caught him looking at old personal photos and videos of them together. I was devastated. The following days at school and work felt dull, forcing myself to sleep each day in a still uncomfortable home. My parents did not seem to want me, and now the person I thought cared for me in the minimal ways he did didn't want me. I felt alone and once again defeated. I didn't talk much about the breakup to my family as I knew they would use that as ammunition to justify that my being gay was not the correct "choice."

You all know the saying, "Time heals everything." It started with the help of someone from my past. I reconnected with my ex from college as friends, and he helped me work through my pain and became an integral part of my healing. A couple of months went by, and my friendship with my ex grew. He became part of my extended family, and we started creating regular plans with my cousins and his friends. My confidence was regaining, and eventually, through these months, I met my now best friend as well. He, too, had gone through a breakup, and we were able to relate to one another despite our age gap. Eventually, I received a drunken phone call in the middle of the night from someone I wasn't expecting: it was Drew.

Confused about why he decided to call me at this hour, I reluctantly answered, knowing I would be asleep. The conversation started with him profusely telling me how much he had missed my company, which quickly turned into him getting angry with me. I can't remember why he got angry, but I do remember that I threatened to hang up the phone if that was the tone he was going to start using with me after breaking up with me two months earlier. He immediately apologized and asked if he could see me to clear the air. I told him we would reconnect later in the day as it was very early in the morning, and I still needed to sleep. Still unsure of what to make of the early morning phone call, I sent him a text message in which he tried to make plans to see me that week. I won't lie; it felt nice to be wanted by someone who didn't want me and realized that they missed my company. But I would find out much later that was not the case.

We met for dinner, during which he told me that he realized he genuinely cared for me and missed me. I thought I was smarter than I was at the time. I told him that he would need to prove to me that he genuinely wanted me in a relationship, but I failed to hold up those boundaries. We went back to his house, where we reconciled the breakup with a very intimate night. The next morning, he told me that he had something to confess.

While we were separated for two months, he had multiple sexual interactions with other people. While we were not together, we failed to get STI checks before being intimate. So, we rushed to the clinic where we got our blood drawn and our mouths swabbed. At this point, I had never had a scare of a possible sexually transmitted infection, and I was quietly praying that my tests would all come back negative.

After a quick 20-minute wait, our test results came back. Mine came back negative, while Drew's came back positive for both gonorrhea and chlamydia. I did not know what to do. At this point, I had just been intimate with him the night before, and his infection results came back positive. The nurse practitioner working at the clinic suggested that since I was intimate with him the night before, it would be in my best interest to get a preventative injection treatment. Not anticipating how painful it would be, I agreed in fear for my health.

That injection was one of the most painful I had ever received. Completing the injection, I immediately grew faint and lost all color in my skin. It took me about 10 minutes before I could get out of the chair and walk out to the lobby. I was extremely disappointed in the person I was calling my partner. Not even 24 hours after we got back together, he had failed me. He knew it.

He immediately tried to raise my spirits and bribe me by grabbing some burgers and fries, which definitely took the sting out of the experience, but that experience left an everlasting imprint on me. However, his desire to win my trust and approval quickly washed away as soon as we started dating again. I immediately sank back into the desire to get his approval when he was the one who told me he wanted me after ending things with me. By this time, I was already of legal drinking age. One of the first gestures he made when we got back together was to take me out to the bars in West Hollywood just to show me around. I was excited and nervous, not knowing what to expect. The first bar we walked into was the infamous Abbey. The music was loud, there were laser lights flashing all over the place, and dancers wearing nothing but speedos or swimwear danced to the music. I felt so overwhelmed, but I wanted to experience this for myself.

As those months passed, we frequented the bars of West Hollywood, or we made sure to buy alcohol at his local grocery store, where we would sit and drink at his home while watching television. This became a common activity for us, but I was blind to the fact that this behavior was unhealthy. After all, I just wanted to spend time with him. I found myself consuming alcohol four times a week, and occasionally, the large bottle of vodka I would purchase at the beginning of the week would be completely empty by Wednesday afternoon.

Drinking alcohol became my escape from my family and from the fact that they did not approve of my sexual orientation, partly because of the unhealthy relationship I was in with Drew. Though my relationship wasn't the healthiest, it allowed me to get out of the house and engage in activities that helped distract me from how I had become the bane of my parents' existence. But it also reminded me of how alone I was in what seemed like this vast gay world.

There were moments when I was frustrated with how hard I worked to prove myself to be an independent, self-sufficient human being by going to school, having a job, and affording all of my personal expenses without bothering my parents. This is what my parents taught me, and that was all they needed from me. Yet, even though I accomplished those things at their minimum, they only chose to see what made them uncomfortable and embarrassed. It was as if I forced them to wear signs that read "My son is gay!" in giant lettering. Not wanting to let these thoughts get me down, I started to pursue expanding my friendships. Now that I was of legal age to drink, my best friend Carlos and I made a plan to go out to the bars. I was nervous about what Drew might think because Carlos was also another gay man, and he had been the jealous type. I reluctantly shared my plans with him, letting him know that I would go out and have drinks with a friend, which was new for me. He immediately began to interrogate me about who this person was, as I had never mentioned him before. Afraid of ruffling feathers, I softly explained that he was my friend and that we planned to go out. He immediately asked how old Carlos was.

Upon finding out how much older Carlos was than me, Drew started to chastise me, telling me that my best friend was only interested in getting in my pants, which was why he would even hang out with me, making his age and orientation the deciding factors for his conclusion.

Essentially, he told me that all I was good for was to be the object of somebody else's desires. That feeling of loneliness sank in, but it was familiar, so I let it be and continued with my plans. I even tried to connect with a new old friend I had met during our initial time apart, trying to make friends at the gym. I happened to meet someone at the gym who was also gay, and we developed a basic level of friendship. We would see each other frequently at the gym, and at one point, we even made plans to hang out with him and his brother at their apartment. During our first and likely last hangout, I noticed they had a bottle of vodka in the shape of a skull on their bar cart, which I had never seen before. Later, I would find out that my inquisitive nature would come back to bite me.

After Drew and I got back together, we went to a local bar in Hollywood for happy hour. I saw the exact same bottle of vodka on the shelf of the bar. I made it a point to share this information with him while we enjoyed some wings and our drinks. He immediately bypassed that information and focused on the fact that I had been at another man's house who was also gay. I tried defending myself, letting him know that we were no longer together at that point and that I was trying to expand my friendship circle. Asserting his possession over me, he threw a tantrum, and we had to leave our happy hour meal immediately. He put me in the car, drove me home, and said, "Don’t call me; I’ll call you,” before speeding off in a rage. At that moment, I didn’t know what to think. I was confused and scared that I would lose the person with whom I had invested emotionally. It was not uncommon for him to get angry, but this was the first time he had told me not to contact him. My anxiety grew as I waited for his phone call, hoping to know that I was in his good graces once again.

It was near the Fourth of July, and I hadn’t received the call. I reached out to him after a week, asking if we could spend time together for the holiday. He agreed, but his demeanor was a little off when I went to see him. Drew, his brother, and his nephew all drove to Santa Barbara to spend the day there and watch the fireworks in the evening. The day started out pretty well. We went to a Mexican restaurant, had a few cocktails, and made our way to the busy beach where everybody was lying out, awaiting the fireworks later that night. While we were sitting on the beach, getting some sun, Drew drunkenly turned over and asked me a very pointed question in a stern tone: “What makes you think that we’re gonna last?” We all know from every dramatic love movie or series that when there is tension between two lovers and alcohol is present, followed by a serious question, it never turns out well. I softly answered, explaining that if we cared about each other enough, we would make this work, no matter what. Clearly, my answer had no positive effect on the situation. His tone grew more enraged as I completed my statement. He grabbed his cup full of alcohol and threw it in my face. Stunned, I quietly got up, rinsed myself off, and let him know that I would take the train from Santa Barbara back to his house, where I would get my car and go home. In the same tone of voice my mother would use to avoid embarrassment in public, he insisted that we needed to fix this and that I was not allowed to leave.

All my clothes were in a plastic bag, and I had put my sunglasses on because I was prepared to leave. As soon as I sat down, he smacked the sunglasses off my face. I immediately started crying. He took my bag of clothes and threw it at me. I did not know how that was supposed to fix anything.

I was at a loss for what to do, but in hindsight, my biggest mistake was not leaving that day. We stayed and watched the fireworks, but even the sight of beautiful lights illuminating the night sky could not change what had transpired earlier. As soon as they were done, we packed up everything and headed to the car. On the car ride home, he became increasingly aggravated with me, completely forgetting that his brother and nephew were in the car.

Somehow, he brought up an old conversation we had a while back that contributed to his frustration, unbeknownst to me. This is when I started to try to assert my boundaries. Once again, he raged and decided to punch me and pinch and poke me until I would give in. Unfortunately, I did, but I quickly realized that the squeaky wheel got more than the grease and that the wheel never stopped squeaking. As soon as we got into his house, he started to panic. Once a man in complete rage, he was now a man in complete fear. He told me he had violated his probation by laying a forceful hand on me.

Now, here's a little backstory. When we first started dating, I asked him about his last relationship, and he told me that they broke up. There was a restraining order on him because, in a drunken rage, he had physically assaulted his boyfriend, and he stated that he never wanted to do that again. I believed him. While he fearfully realized he had violated court-ordered probation, smoking his cigarette, he begged me not to call the cops on him for punching me.

It's not something I initially thought of, so I was caught off guard when he asked me not to do so. He then immediately said that we needed to go to couples counseling.

Knowing that I would get an earful from my mother, I kept it a secret. My mother could barely stand that her son was gay; I was not about to subject her to my relationship problems. Upon getting to the LGBTQ center, where we would meet the person to help us mend our relationship, Drew turned to me in the car and, in a stern voice, told me not to say anything about him hitting me to the therapist. I thought therapy was a place where honesty could flourish, but clearly, it was where Drew dictated what I was allowed to share as long as it didn't make him look bad. However, upon sitting in the room with the therapist, he had no issues making me seem like the crazy one. After that first session, I could not shake the fact that my partner made me out to be the crazy one to a stranger while my parents saw me as the crazy one for "choosing" this life for myself. I couldn't help but wonder if this was all worth it.

Over the course of the six months we were in therapy, we did the same dance, and it didn't seem like we made much progress. There were also moments when he would cut me down for the sake of it. During this time, I was still figuring out what I wanted to do with my life. Upon feeling like the junior college system had failed me, I turned to online schooling, where I decided to pursue a Bachelor's degree in nutrition sciences. Once Drew found out, he chuckled and, under his breath, said I wouldn't be successful at establishing a career with that degree. This was coming from a man who was 26 years old, had no degree, and had been collecting unemployment since I met him. We did, however, vacation frequently in Vegas, and we would have a great time, but only on the condition that I would pay for the hotel if I wanted to participate. Thankfully, we had a friend who would want to join, and when he came, Drew knew we would never have to pay for much and would most likely stay at the nicest hotel since our friend was a frequent high-stakes gambler.

The day of our second-to-last therapy session would be our last. Unfortunately, my confiding in my old college lover turned friend was a no-no. Somehow, that grapevine grew its way to Drew, and I got an earful before he broke up with me. Of course, I was sad, but this time I felt a little different. I was older and had started to establish my life outside of my relationship, so it stung a little less. At this time, I still was not sharing my dating life with my family, so no one knew he had ended things with me for the second time.

On one particular night out, I had gone to West Hollywood with some friends for a much-needed time out. After walking into the loud club, my future self immediately saw my past. There he was, one drink in each hand, and he wasn't happy when I spotted him. I worked up the confidence to say "hi." My logic was that if I let him know I was there, I wouldn't worry about whether he would see me. After a quick greeting, he sped off into the light show of the dance floor, and I continued on with my night without issue. I ended my night and felt a presence behind me as I was leaving the club. In a drunken mess, Drew swooped up behind me and loudly said in my ear, "You know I don't like seeing you out!" Having liquid courage in my system, I would not let him get away with that statement. There I was on Santa Monica Blvd, just as messy as he was, but with my words. I had seen couples argue on the street before, but I never thought I would be that person. My friends quickly brought the car around and rushed me into it, and I went home for the night.

Later that week, I got an apology text from Drew. I was fed up with him. How could someone who insults me one minute seek my forgiveness, knowing very well that this was not the first occurrence? It felt similar to my experiences with my parents, where unreasonable actions collided with my reasonable mind, yet I was the problem. In his message, he begged to apologize by taking me to dinner and saying he wanted to talk it out. Reluctantly, I obliged. As I sat at dinner, my hard, confident exterior quickly became a soft pile of mush when I said the words, "I missed you," followed by his pathetic explanation for his outburst that night and him asking for another chance.

The question I've asked myself for years is: why did I continue with this unhealthy relationship? Was it because I was desperate to feel love from someone since I did not feel it from the people who mattered most to me? Or was I just a naïve young gay man still learning to walk in this crazy gay world? Either way, that question was not answered or asked, and I gave Drew another shot. Hoping things would change, I found myself back to where I started: a man who got the toy he had begged to have and was bored with it a few weeks later. Though I didn't get the boot after the boredom, he had an unconventional way to keep me engaged. One evening, as we were partaking in our typical activity—drinking cocktails that were way too strong in cups way too big while watching television—I heard a faint call for his name in the other room from his mother. He darted out to see what she needed and didn't come back into the room for quite some time. When he did, I could sense something had changed. With his "you did something wrong" attitude, he asked me, "Is there something you want to tell me?" Confused, I repeated his question back. He then confessed that his mom had lost some money from her dresser drawer—$70 to be exact. She had consulted a psychic from El Salvador who had told her some vague reading that turned into "Jonathan came into the bedroom, opened the dresser, and stole the money." He blindly believed his mother and started to accuse me of theft. Stunned at the dramatic turn the evening took, I stormed out of his house and made my way back to my parents' house. Somehow, a home where "I love you" was put on hold seemed more comfortable than a home where I was now painted as a thief.

Frustrated, I had messed up Drew by saying my piece. Offended that someone who had never shown a disrespectful bone in his body was now looking at me in the most disrespectful light, I felt betrayed. But that was the problem. According to his mother, she understood why I would have taken the money. I had given her a Mother's Day gift and a blender for her birthday due to a hand injury. My generosity incriminated me with both her and Drew. Throughout my coming-out process, I had made sure not to ruffle the feathers of anyone in the line of fire. I was also pleading my case with my parents, who thought I was rarely home because of my participation in illegal drug use and excessive drinking. Now, I wouldn't say the drinking part was a total lie, but I wasn't drinking more than anyone my age was at the time. Somehow, I was the villain to two groups of people: my parents and my boyfriend.

Thankfully, that situation blew over, but I couldn't shake the feeling that I wasn't as welcome in Drew's home as I had been before. My trust in Drew was definitely tested after that. He suddenly started to act a tad more cocky than usual. I finally figured out why. One afternoon, we went to grab food from a new food truck that had popped up and brought it back to his home. As I walked out of the bathroom, ready to eat my fill, I saw his iPod touch on the counter, unlocked and open to a well-known gay dating app, Grindr. In utter shock at why my partner, whom I thought I was monogamous with, would be online with a grid of different shirtless men, I asked him what that was about. His response was, "You can't get mad at me for that." It was as if I had no right to question his actions at that moment. He then spouted out some excuse that I later decided wasn't worth the fight.

Some time went on, and we wound up with the same predicament as months prior: he was breaking up with me again. I took it much better than the first two times, and through experience, I warned him that he would see me out, which he seemed fine with. I was sad, but I was also content with the decision.

At this time, I had been out for about two years and had finally started to open up to my parents. Though they tolerated my sharing of experiences, they didn't say much to support me. Even though our relationship was nowhere near where it used to be, there would be a pivotal moment that forced us to call a truce, at least for a little while. My grandmother had a stroke. This woman had been in my life from the start. She lived with us during my later years in high school, helping with laundry, cooking, cleaning, and being the lovely woman she was. Her stroke had landed her in the hospital, which then progressed to her having Alzheimer's and dementia. Based on the diagnosis, she would need constant care. Given that I was in an online college program and working part-time while my brother was away in the military, I was the natural choice to help out. I became a state trainer and legal caregiver. Once again, being placed in a parent-child role, I had more responsibility than I could manage, but it was worth it. I got to take care of my grandmother, and the state would pay me to do it. As a broke college student, I appreciated the compensation. My mother and I laid out the agreement, and upon accepting the responsibility, I noticed my mother was also being compensated. If you're unaware of the process, the state gives you a timecard every two weeks with allotted hours that can be claimed. You fill that out and send it in, and they submit a paycheck for the time. Between my mother and me, we had split about 200 hours, with my mom writing more time on her card than I did. Little did I realize that I would be doing 90% of the work since she had to go to work, and I was the only one left home with my grandmother. My duties included bathing her, feeding her, getting her dressed for the day, nurse visits, and occasionally taking her to adult daycare for some social time. I was quite literally a parent to this woman. But we will get to my grandmother later on.

During this process, being in a very vulnerable state, Drew managed to weasel his way back into my life and we started dating again. A couple of months went by, and it was the holidays. Our mutual friend was getting ready to celebrate his 40th birthday, and in classic fashion, it would be done in Vegas. Planning on going, we weren't in the best spirits as Drew would start a fight with me, which, at this point, I was used to. We had gone on a little shopping trip to get some clothes to wear for this event. Later on, I found out that I had been disinvited, specifically by the birthday boy. I assumed that Drew would not attend if I didn't go in solidarity. That was not the case. In fact, he seemed happy that I wasn't going, which then caused more of a stir between us. Sitting in my thoughts, I asked myself again how much more I would tolerate feeling like a doormat to someone who claims to have feelings for me.

Pondering what I should do next, I was quickly reminded that I was loved. Not by my partner, but by someone who slowly forgot who I was: my grandmother. This woman, who would get too frustrated when she couldn't find the words, who was bashful every time I had to bathe her, yet smiled in excitement every morning as I got her out of bed or picked her up from the adult daycare, loved me. That smile on her face helped me make my decision. That weekend, he had gone to Vegas. I did not message him the entire weekend until Monday morning, when I had made my choice. As soon as he landed, he called me, and I worked up the courage to let him know that I was not able to continue the relationship. Confused and enraged, he sped over to my house and parked his car on the street. He did not get out of the car, so I continued to speak to him on the phone to explain myself. Once I finished, he sped off, and I hadn't heard from him since.

Part III

My parents were so relieved that I had ended this chaotic, toxic relationship. But the toxicity did not stop there. Subsequently, I jumped into another relationship. Thankfully, by this time, I had made some friends in the gay community who helped me work through some of my issues from the last one. But I was about to embark on another unexpected learning experience. His name was Alvie. We had met in tandem during the end of my last relationship. Our first date was not conventional. Prior to our first date, he disclosed that he was not out to any of his family members. Having been in his position, I empathized with him and proceeded to plan our first date. He had set an evening for us, but given it was the holiday season, he had a family engagement he had to attend, which he invited me to. Yes, I met the entire family upon meeting this person for the first time. Talk about being overwhelmed. When I got to his house, he introduced me to his family as a classmate from Cal Berkeley. The only time I had ever stepped foot on that campus was for a campus tour years earlier with my friend.

There was a traditional nativity reenactment, followed by singing, and then Alvie and I would leave for our official date. He was a low-key guy with a calm demeanor, which was the opposite of my last relationship. It was refreshing. After a couple of months of secret dinner and cocktail dates, he asked me if I would want to pursue him more seriously. I reluctantly answered, "yes," as I wasn't sure if jumping into something so quickly with my family and friends would look bad. My parents disliked my lifestyle, and my friends were very opinionated, given I was the youngest in the group. I ultimately received blessings from my friends, and my parents came around shortly after they met Alvie.

Alvie and I operated pretty cohesively for the most part. I would always be invited to his family functions, as his cousins loved my company, and I always came with some form of food as a sign of respect for his inviting me. The only rub in this situation was that we were not allowed to display affection when we were around his family since no one knew about us. However, my sexuality was made abundantly clear. I wasn't too bothered with this initially because it started to feel like things were falling into place. My parents were more comfortable with me, though on occasion, my mother would throw out the comment that she wished I would end up with a woman and gift her a grandchild. My father and I did not have the most engaging relationship aside from the basic greetings and requests for help with chores or tasks in my free time. What won my parents over was that Alvie would occasionally help me out with my grandmother since he worked from his cousin's home office, 10 minutes from my house.

Things slowly got challenging as my patience with him coming out wore thin, and my fear of what he was up to after I went to bed grew stronger; he was a night owl, so his bedtime was well after I went to sleep. I hated being a secret when he was no secret in my life. He partly disclosed that if he came out, he could be cut off from any financial assistance from his family since he worked for his family and lived at home. At one point, I needed a break to collect myself. I wasn't afraid to speak my mind at this point. Keep in mind that I had just gotten out of a toxic relationship where my cognitive distortion was exacerbated. But now, similarly, it was brought to the surface for a different reason.

If you are unaware of what cognitive distortion is, it's an exaggerated or irrational thought that is caused by perceived reality rather than actual reality. If you have cognitive distortion, you may be someone who catastrophizes things. For example, you may have gotten the time wrong for an event, and upon finding out, you develop anxiety thinking about the worst-case scenario rather than accepting it was a simple mistake. You could be someone who minimizes things, thinking that what positive experiences you have are not deserved or that someone else deserves them over you.

Like myself, you may be an emotional reasoner, thinking with your heart and not your head based on how you feel. As poetic as that may sound, it does not always lead to anyone's benefit. There are other traits that can classify cognitive distortion. But if you are concerned about it, know that it is a learned pattern of thinking that can be unlearned with the right tools. Sometimes, we are unaware of this patterning, as some of these thought processes were learned from childhood and have been a fact of life for us.

In this relationship, I found myself jumping to conclusions at any action that seemed out of place, along with the other characteristics I possessed. At that time, I did not think I was dealing with cognitive distortion. In fact, I did not even know that term back then. I thought I was a well-adjusted person who had just some minor trust issues that were justified due to my ability to explain myself. Later, I learned that just because you can justify an action or a feeling does not always make it right or factual reality.

Once I was able to cool off I ask Alvie if he would want to continue dating, he was totally fine with that. But something would come back from my past to trigger me once again. While we were on a break, he had downloaded Grindr; dating app usually meant for singles to meet, that I was not keen on him having the app now that we were back together. He explained that he used it to make friends since he did not have gay friends of his own. I replayed my last experience in my head and did not want to feel stupid for letting this slide the way I did before. I sat him down and said that if he wanted to keep it, there would be some rules to make me more comfortable with him having it. He willingly accepted my request, and all was well—or so I thought. My parents, having liked Alvie, did not have any problems with him coming by and staying the night. On one of those nights, he shared that he had made a new friend. He disclosed their prior conversations on the app as well as other interactions he had. At this time, we had agreed to share access to each other's cell phones since trust was a big thing to me. Not thinking much of it, I went about the evening.

It was not until he decided to officially meet this person that I noticed a change in his attitude toward our agreement and our open line of communication. On the day of his meeting with his new friend, I was staying over at his house since his family was away. We figured it would be a great opportunity for us to have quality time together without our families roaming around. He had left in the morning for a hike, with a "friend" from Grindr and I just went about my Saturday tidying up the house and getting groceries to make dinner. Hours had gone by, and I had not heard from Alvie. I started to feel uncomfortable at his parents' house, all alone while he was out meeting some guy on a dating app. It had been a total of eight hours since he had left, and he finally came back to the house. I was furious. He explained how the hike turned into lunch and that time got away from them. But it started to sound and feel like it was a date more than anything. My trust in him started to fade. I was now back where I did not want to be. He was quick to defend his actions, which only gave me the impression that he was guilty of something. I had a gut feeling that this person was up to no good.

A few weeks passed, and he was overspending the night as usual, but a part of me could not shake the feeling that something was off. He wanted to shower after being at the gym and left his phone on my desk. We all know where this is going. I unlocked his phone and opened the dating app to see what activity he had been up to, making sure not to open any unread messages, as he would know someone had gone onto the app. I then went through his photo album to see if he had any incriminating evidence of inappropriate activity. It's true what they say: "If you look for something, you will find it." I did. Right there in his album, he had taken explicit photos of himself smirking in the mirror, as if he was sending them to someone in real time. Thankfully, iPhones time-stamped when photos were taken, so I knew that it was done earlier that week at 2:15 a.m. Containing my rage, I waited until he got out of the shower and addressed the photos in a calm tone. I asked if those were for anyone, and he replied, "No." Knowing it was a lie, I jokingly said, "I'm going to send these to myself since I want to have them for myself." He didn't object.

I wasn't sure what to do. My parents slowly started to come around and liked Alvie, yet I did not feel safe in that relationship. I felt like I was in an alternate version of my previous relationship. I was triggered by the fact that in my last relationship I was made to feel guilty for feeling upset about my partner being on an app meant for single individuals. Even when I knew my rationale was valid I was made to believe I was out of place. It started to feel all too familiar.

After some reassurance from Alvie about the situation, I was able to let it go for a while. Months went by, and it was the holiday season. I was working a seasonal position at Lululemon, which I enjoyed because of the hourly compensation and the discounts on their athletic clothing. It was Black Friday, one of the busiest times for retail, and I had a private personal training client in the morning. Unfortunately, I had strained my back with my client and did not think much of it. I walked into my shift at the store ready to go, but my back started to tense up within the first couple of hours of my shift.

During my lunch break, I texted Alvie about the unfortunate situation, and he agreed to come by and be a supportive partner later that night after he hung out with his friend, whom I wasn't the most comfortable with. However, I did not want to start an argument, so I let him be. I finished my shift and went home to decompress. As soon as I lay down on my bed, my back seized up immediately, making any movement excruciatingly painful. I texted Alvie to let him know it had gotten worse, but he was still at his hangout.

As 11:30 p.m. rolled around, which was the time he said he would come over, I had not heard anything from him. Midnight came about, and I decided to give him a call. He answered in a confused tone, wondering why I was calling him. In pain and frustration, I sternly asked when he was planning to come by since it was now an hour past his initial arrival time. He started to gaslight me, making me feel as if I had no right to be angry with him, and proceeded to tell me he no longer wanted to come by and that he would finish out his night with his friend.

At this point, I was able to vent to my mother, who seemed supportive until she made remarks about how, if I was with a girl, this would never be an issue. Then she justified herself by saying she only cared about my well-being. I felt at odds with both Alvie and my mother in this situation. At this time, I decided to reach out to the therapist who helped me in my previous relationship to get a second opinion on what I should be doing. After four expensive sessions, I concluded that this relationship was past its expiration date, and I was just holding on to what could be versus what really was. I realized that 1) Alvie would never come out to his family for me, and 2) I was in his first gay relationship. He had a lot to explore and learn that I could not, nor wanted to, teach him.

Once the deed was done, I was hyper-focused on my grandmother and graduating college. I needed to ensure my exit from my parents' house, which I eventually did after my grandmother passed away. I was able to secure a full-time position working for a luxury big-box gym. I quickly became the number one grossing personal trainer on staff, working about 150 to 200 hours per month. I did not know what that meant since I was used to working many hours without seeing much monetary success. Once I received my first paycheck after a full pay period of training with a full calendar, I was shocked. I had made more in two weeks than what I used to make in three months. My confidence and morale grew, washing away the stress that was at home or in my romantic life. This was my priority now. I was so excited to show my parents that their son was becoming something of himself they could be proud of, and I regretfully showed them my first paycheck. My decision to over share about my success was not met with the reaction I had anticipated. Though they were mildly surprised of my success

my mother was not comfortable with how busy I had gotten, calling me during training sessions and yelling at me for not being home at a certain hour. I remember there was one instance when I was training my last client of the day at 7 p.m. Sessions were about an hour, which would have me finish at 8 p.m. and most likely be home before 9 p.m. During my session, my mother called me and angrily asked why I was not home. When I responded with, "I'm at work training," she immediately questioned the validity of my answer, saying, "People really work this late?"

Frustrated, I said I had to go and quickly hung up the phone to complete my service. My mom, being so used to my presence at home, had a hard time with me finally detaching. While working for this gym, I made friends among my peers but got close with two of the girls. One of them was in the middle of a housing transition and needed a room to rent, so I offered the spare room at my parents' house. I enjoyed her company, and my mother did not mind the extra $400 per month. My mom was still not fully happy with my sexual orientation, but she kept it to herself most of the time. One night, while I was out and my coworker—now my housemate—was at home, my mom approached her in confidence, asking if she would try and "make Jonathan hers." She uncomfortably laughed and discussed with my mom that it would be impossible for that to happen, as being gay isn't about choice or being swayed. As soon as I got home, my coworker immediately decided we needed to look for an apartment, knowing that the environment was unhealthy.

Part IV

After moving out of my parents' home, it seemed like my relationship with them got harder. I would try to make time to visit, but it would result in an argument and me storming out of the house and back to my apartment. This was our dynamic for a while, with some glimpses of positive, enjoyable visits. During this time, I was pretty quiet about dating. I feared the judgment from my parents after years of it with my last two relationships. Many apartments and a job later, I met someone. We belonged to the same gym, which is where we both initially noticed one another. One evening, I saw him on my personal social media page and decided to "slide into his DMs," as we millennials would say. At first, I did not know if he was gay and was suggesting harmless workouts together at the gym. He then suggested we grab brunch, which made it clear he was interested in me more than just as a workout buddy.

We exchanged pleasantries and found out we both shared the same name. To avoid confusion, we will just call him Jon. Jon and I took to one another very quickly. This was a dating experience I had never felt, though I was much older and wiser now. We spent a lot of time together, and due to unexpected circumstances, Jon ended up moving into my apartment after six weeks of dating. I was nervous yet excited, as I had never lived with a significant other before.

Somehow, we both logistically lucked out. We had a lot of similarities in how we liked to keep our living spaces and very few differences on that front. After a month of confidence-building living together with Jon, it was time to meet the parents. His mother lived in another state, so I never got to meet her in person. We picked a Sunday and went to brunch. Jon was nervous, and so was I. In the past, whenever my parents met someone new, they didn't give the most welcoming impression. It usually took a while for them to warm up to someone. But to my surprise, it was a smooth meeting, and they seemed to enjoy his company. So, we regularly planned family dinners with my parents.

During this time, I transitioned from fitness training to teaching high school, which included a massive pay cut. I was financially challenged every month after paying all of my bills and purchasing the essentials. After sharing this with Jon, he said he was willing to help pick up the slack since he was making more than I was. I rarely asked my parents for financial assistance, but during this time, I had asked for some help with groceries here and there. My mom kept a mental tally of every time she had given me money and threw it back in my face whenever we had an argument. While I was with Jon, my mom made a comment when we were arguing that Jon was spending all my money, which is why I seemed broke all the time. I did not know how she deduced that with little to no knowledge of our relationship.

It was funny how, in one minute, my mother would say how much she liked someone and then villainize them in the next breath. Jon and I had our usual relationship issues, but this started to add to that. This made Jon not want to participate in family dinner nights or big family events, which, in turn, frustrated me because he was not in the picture. This bothered me because once he stopped showing up to family events, the good qualities my mother once noticed about him faded, and he truly became the villain.

Jon and I started to have deeper issues in our relationship when we realized we had moved in with one another too quickly. The similarities that were once so apparent slowly became differences; insecurities grew, and communication turned into defining silence.

This was all in a matter of eight months. Desperate to make things work, I allowed Jon to skip family functions and made excuses for him so my family would ease up on their judgment. I did my best to respect what he needed. Eventually, the topic of getting a dog came into play, as months before, we had taken care of the family dog, and he loved it. For the following two months, all he could talk about was how he saw individuals with their K9 companions at work. Having had dogs before, I knew what the challenges were, not to mention that he wanted a puppy to raise, which comes with its own set of challenges.

After a few months of back and forth, I surprised him with a visit to an animal foundation. We had settled on a breed, and they had puppies available. Once entering the foundation's adoption event, we chatted with a staff member about the puppies they had advertised.

Unfortunately, they were all adopted out early that morning, but their mother was still there. We asked to see the mother. She was a beautiful blue-nosed brindle pit bull. She put her paw up on the cage as we approached her, and we immediately asked if we could play with her. She was no puppy, but we knew she was meant to be ours. So, we filled out all the paperwork and waited patiently until she was ready to be released. We named her Lila.

Lila became a mutual interest for us both. We had cuddle piles with her, family outings, and even a few mischievous accidents that seemed to bring Jon and me closer together. Things started to look brighter. I developed a routine for my new job, and Jon was working on getting a promotion. We eventually discussed getting an updated apartment since my lease was about to end. As much as we wanted to move immediately, we had one issue: Lila was considered a restricted breed. Most buildings would deny us the ability to apply because we owned a pit bull.

While Jon was away for training, I kept looking and found an apartment that was updated to our liking, and the landlady had no issues with Lila. I brought her to the viewing so she could meet her firsthand. Excitedly, I texted Jon and told him about the unit, and he eagerly wanted to see it. When he got back from his trip, we went to the unit as soon as possible. Within minutes of him seeing the unit, he said, "Yes." That marked the beginning of a new chapter in our lives.

Once we moved into our apartment, things didn't get better as anticipated. It seemed that the problems we tried to leave behind followed us to our new home, and Lila, who seemed to have brought us together, became my responsibility. I now had more rent and more to worry about.

Our sex life was sparse, leaving me feeling like I wasn't enough. My insecurities grew once again, but I did not make the mistake of oversharing, as it had landed Jon and me in arguments in the past. Given that our expenses grew, I needed my income to grow. I was tired of Jon stating that I was not making enough money and that the way the district paid teachers was not on the most convenient schedule. So, on top of my duties at home and my main job, I took on a second job to make up for the difference in our incomes as much as possible. Similarly, when I got my first major paycheck, I shared my new earnings with Jon. In an uninterested tone, he said, "Nice," and went about his day. I felt minimized in my relationship; my success or feelings weren't big enough because our differences became bigger.

There were some glimmers of hope here and there, but those quickly faded once an argument arose. There was one instance when the argument was so bad I found myself crying on the phone to my mother, asking if I could stay at the house. The stain of that argument lasted weeks. I had now found myself back in a familiar situation where I was walking on eggshells in my own home, trying not to disturb the calm yet uninviting environment. Eventually, we were able to come to a resolution, but I think it was simply the fact that we both did not know what to do but wanted to keep the peace.

Months later, I decided that we should go on a little vacation. I had planned for a dog sitter, and it would be with my best friend and his partner at the time. Unfortunately, as the trip neared, Jon said he could not make it, and the trip quickly turned into a best friend getaway. After my three-day getaway, I somehow got sick in the following days. Jon was attentive but not in the way he used to be. It was more robotic and sterile. I sensed something was wrong but kept quiet, thinking I was making it all up in my head. Later that week, we went out to dinner with some friends, and since it was close to our home, we walked back. I still had the feeling that something was off, and on our walk, I worked up the courage to address it. He shared his disinterest in our relationship while I was away with my best friend and concluded the conversation with words I did not expect to hear: "I don't love you anymore."

Angry, sad, confused, and jolted, I did not know how to react. I was emotionless and immediately asked what our next step was. We both decided to take a step back and revisit this subject later. A week later, we officially called it quits. Having just been in our new home for six months, I was too stubborn to leave. I stayed in that one-bedroom apartment, sharing the space with Jon. I was secretly hoping he would try again, but that never happened. What I did get was an occasional earful when I came home late from a night out being single.

Similarly to my experience with my mom, in one moment I would be the best person in their life, and the next, they could not bear to see me happy without them. It has been said that a true person's personality will shine in the presence of adversity. It was clear that when Jon and I got into an argument, he would burst into a rage, followed by the silent treatment. After three months, I had no desire to continue living in that environment, but I was still financially obligated to live in the apartment. I'm not going to lie; living under my mother's roof felt more like a piece of cake than this situation. So I decided to leave the apartment. My mom was supportive yet frustrated since she had converted my room into her office/fitness room. I packed up what was mine in the apartment and left.

Upon planning my exit, I was trying to figure out a solution for Lila, but unfortunately, my parents would not let me keep her, given her size. Having worked longer hours than me, Jon felt terrible about having created her for longer than he wanted. So we made the hardest choice, which was to rehome her. Though we physically separated from one another, Jon and I still needed to stay in contact for the duration of the lease term. I was preoccupied with getting myself settled, doing a bodybuilding show, and working, so my communication was limited to when it was necessary. It was fine for a time, but I was distracting myself from grieving the end of my relationship. With teaching students for six hours a day, plus an additional three hours of fitness daily on top of meal prepping and making additional income with fitness training, I found myself asking questions that led to dead ends.

Eventually, I was able to take all I had learned and move forward with my life, with more confidence and reassurance that I was where I needed to be.

Chapter 4: The Parentified Grandson

In most immigrant families, children often grow up faster than the average American child. While most American kids are enjoying their youth, playing outside, or getting into mischief, immigrant children are learning how to be adults—whether that is caring for their younger siblings or grandparents, learning the family trade, or just helping keep the house up. This can vary based on many factors that can cause this to happen. In many cases immigrants come with little to no establishment in the USA, hoping for a better life and raising children in the midst of this uproot. In many cultures, the purpose of having children is that when parents get older, they will be taken care of. That doesn't mean parents love their children any less because of this expectation; in fact, it comes from a place of great care, but they have already enlisted them in duties that children are not emotionally prepared for. This term is called parentification, which I had briefly stated in chapter 2. Parentification or parent child is when parents look to their children for emotional and practical support that children are not yet prepared for. This can look like a child being forced to work to help support their family which looks different thana teenager deciding to get a part time job to have some financial freedom.

In most cases, parentified children are drawn into their parents' issues, such as financial problems and marital strife; they thrive in situations of crisis or chaos, feeling responsible for their parents' well-being along with other burdens that children are not mentally prepared to take on. That was the case for me growing up. After a certain age, my parents stopped treating my brother and me as kids and started teaching us lessons on how to be adults. We were taught the value of money at a young age and made aware of my parents' financial stresses and health issues as we got older. I was only 16 years old when I got my first job because I was convinced I needed to add more value to my family. The desire to play a more valuable role in my home only grew from then on. With how our household was run, I started to feel a specific obligation to be helpful to my family, thinking that it would somehow diminish my insecurity. But there was one elderly person from whom I never felt pressured.

My loving grandmother was everything to me. She was the one constant person in my life, someone I always found by my side. She was so caring and loving. She was there for me at every step of my life and was my biggest cheerleader. She always ensured that we were cared for in the best ways possible. She cared for every little thing, no matter how small or insignificant, whether it was sewing us pajamas to wear to sleep or feeding us home-cooked meals every time we came to see her or she came to see us. She never denied doing laundry for us or even taught us fun little trades.

For me specifically, my grandmother taught me how to sew and basic life etiquette. There were a couple of times when I wanted to alter something in my wardrobe, and she would just come and do it for me. She did this out of love, without questioning or teaching me how to do it myself. She never really demanded much from her grandkids; instead, she always showed support, aside from the occasional request to take her to the grocery store, where she would, without warning or question, hand you a $20 bill for your troubles. Unlike my parents, who always seemed to request favors for access to do things, she never really asked anything of us. She was a gem of a person, always enjoying these favors out of the goodness of her heart.

As time passed and she got older, her health started deteriorating. She ended up having two strokes back-to-back, which was alarming for all of us. We were so worried for her, as the strokes were only about a week apart. She stayed in the hospital until she recovered completely. When she finally came back from the hospital after the second stroke, the doctor revealed that the strokes had affected some parts of her brain. Thus, she was diagnosed with progressive Alzheimer's and dementia. Due to this, she experienced memory loss and her speech was slightly affected. She lost the ability to communicate effectively, as some words were hard for her to think of or sound out. This happens with damage or disruptions in brain areas that control spoken language. She became distraught over losing her ability to speak. She used to communicate in English, but after the stroke, she only spoke in her mother tongue, Arabic. She would get frustrated because, despite several attempts, she couldn't remember the words. You could see the frustration on her face as she tried to have a conversation or explain what she wanted from the kitchen; the words simply wouldn't come. It was a new language I would have to learn to make life a little easier.

During her discharge from the hospital, the doctors expressed their concern. They told us that she would no longer be able to live on her own, which was a concern for us. It was devastating news because she was the person who always enjoyed doing her chores herself. The doctors declared that she would need constant care and supervision from now on. I listened to this conversation, worried for her. Amidst the shock, my mom asked me for the biggest favor yet—to become her legal caregiver. Now, I wasn't her only child, but it was obvious that she couldn't ask my brother because he was away in the military. I also had extended family; there were various aunts and uncles and many cousins as well, but all of them were busy with their lives. One cousin was in college overseas, and the other two were busy with their personal careers and relationships, though they would visit from time to time, which we all enjoyed.

Therefore, I was the only one who could be the best fit for the caretaker role. My mom assumed my schedule was much more relaxed than it was since I was in online school and had a part-time job. She thought it wouldn't be a big deal and that I would manage all of the tasks perfectly. It wasn't uncommon for my parents to assume I could handle any stressful task they didn't have the bandwidth for. At that time, I didn't have a full-time career and was still in school. My part-time job wasn't seen as a high priority, and my parents seemed to think I was always wasting my time and money on myself when I could be doing something more productive.

When my mom asked me to be her legal caregiver, I was nervous about accepting because I'd never taken care of another human being in the same way that she needed care. I also had no experience and was reluctant to accept the offer. As a young adult of only 22, I was busy figuring out my life path and keeping my head above water. How could I manage this responsibility? I was already juggling minimum payments on my credit card, which was quite challenging. And then came the responsibility of taking care of a 90-year-old woman who would essentially forget a lot of things. I was afraid I couldn't bear the weight of the responsibility of caring for an elderly woman, being so young, irresponsible, and naive.

However, my mom convinced me by saying that the state of California would pay me to take care of her as long as I completed the proper training, which I had done, and I would receive help from my mother. I was desperate to make extra money at the time because I wasn't able to pay for basic necessities without maxing out my credit cards. I was broke and scared, not wanting to take on the responsibility, but somehow I accepted the request. After an 8-hour training day, I became my grandmother's legal caregiver. However, I wasn't prepared for the responsibility I was going to undertake for her.

Throughout her life, she did so much for me. I was emotionally invested in her well-being. It was time to reverse the roles. My routine started with waking her up every morning, walking her to the bathroom, bathing her, and keeping her clean and tidy so she wouldn't get an infection. She was like a little child who needed reminders to eat and take her medicine on time. I was there to feed her and make sure she took her medication and didn't sneak it out of her mouth and spit it out, which she often did. I had to watch her closely to ensure she took all her medications. I treated her like a naughty child who hated taking medicine, so we turned it into a little game to make the challenging task more fun, and I got a few laughs out of her at the same time. Occasionally, when I had to work, I would take her to an adult daycare center to participate in activities and socialize. Though it was hard to see this confused and defenseless woman leave for a few hours, I knew it had to be done. I loved seeing her excited face when I picked her up and took her to get one of her favorite meals, a cheeseburger and fries. I ensured she was comfortable with everything around her.

During this time, I also found myself responsible for overseeing all of my grandmother's nursing visits, which included checking her vitals, taking her blood, and following up on her care. Unfortunately, she ended up in the hospital a couple of times due to accidental injuries she caused unintentionally. The social workers often called me because

I was her legal caregiver and held the responsibility for her well-being. I didn't fully understand the extent of my responsibilities until I was thrust into this role. Eventually, I managed to establish a routine that allowed me to handle everything that needed to be done. And that's how the days passed. Though I felt a personal responsibility to help my grandmother, it was a lot to handle mentally and emotionally.

After a few months, I began to feel like I was missing out on my early twenties, and the pressure started weighing on me. I realized that I couldn't make bad decisions. I couldn't be carefree or stay out late with my friends because I had to wake up early the next day to care for another person. Selfishly, I was getting frustrated that I couldn't just go out and hang out with my friends like I used to, without the fear that if I wasn't there for my grandmother, something could happen to her. Several times, I requested additional support from my parents to have more time for myself, but that conversation was quickly shut down and brushed aside, leading to some future animosity. I was immediately triggered by my past experience of taking care of my brother. The feeling of helplessness and frustration washed over me.

I felt like I was about to crack. I pleaded for their aid in tears, and once again, I was quickly shut down and told there was no need to cry. I shouldered a noteworthy amount of responsibility while my parents were at work, and I felt that I wasn't receiving fair compensation for my efforts or any additional assistance when I needed it. Not only was I assigned to care for another individual, but I also felt unrecognized and underpaid, as if my work was being taken for granted.

When it came time for my mother and me, who shared the financial benefits of being her legal caregiver, there was a clear discrepancy in how many hours I reported versus how many hours she reported. For those who don't know about caregiving services, it works like this: when you are a legal caregiver, you are given a certain number of monthly hours by the state you're allowed to use, which are split up weekly on time cards. Whenever my mother and I did our timesheets, my mom would always seem to add more hours to hers, which would yield her more money, while I would not. I would add in the number she specified that I should add because if I added any more, she wouldn't be able to add any to hers. This started to create a little bit of resentment.

How was I doing most of the work while juggling my other responsibilities and not being respected or compensated for my time and efforts? While in college, I dedicated myself to caring for my grandmother. Her safety and happiness were my top priorities. This involved balancing my studies with part-time work to supplement my income. It was a challenging but rewarding experience for me. I was only making about $400 every two weeks, while my mom made around $1,000 every two weeks. I tried to reason with my mother and ask if there was any way she could spare me a few more hours, as I was doing the majority of the workload. She immediately threw a fit and started calling me selfish and ungrateful. She tried to convince me that the excess money was used for my grandmother's bills, though I saw no bills in her name. At that time, her particular insurance covered the majority of all expenses.

My frustration grew; I was not happy with where things were going. This behavior felt like a betrayal to me. I felt as if my family was using me and leveraging the fact that I was their child and that they brought me into this world to be helpful and not to be more of a burden. As much as I wanted to stop doing it altogether, I felt obligated to this woman who couldn't remember my name because of her progressing dementia. It made me realize that, at that time, my value system relied on how many individuals I could support and care for. But while doing that, I did not take care of myself. I left myself under piles of responsibilities. I did not realize the detriment it would have on my mental health, causing me to seek approval from individuals outside of my family.

Basically, I was overworked and stressed out because of the ongoing situation, but I was determined to try and salvage a little amusement in my life. It was 2013; I was invited to go to a music festival in Las Vegas. The drive from Los Angeles to Las Vegas is about four hours. When we arrived in Vegas, I found myself in a situation where I didn't have enough money to purchase tickets for the entire weekend event; I wondered why.

As a result, I ended up in Vegas on my own while my partner at the time, along with his extended family and friends, was at the festival. It wasn't until the final evening that I finally had the opportunity to experience and enjoy the festival fully. I boarded that trip, even though I was fully aware that I needed to be back in Los Angeles by seven o'clock Monday morning. I wanted to make sure I could wake my grandmother up, get her fed, and help her get dressed. This was necessary because she attended adult daycare a few times a week, allowing her to engage in social interactions and participate in activities outside the house.

So, we went to this music festival, which started at 7 p.m. Sunday night. After having a great time at the music festival, my partner and I ended up staying until 2:30 in the morning, which was when the DJ my partner wanted to see would end. As the night came to a close, we began packing our bags and loading them into the car. We knew we needed to hit the road back to Los Angeles to fulfill a responsibility I had committed to.

Even though I was able to attend the event, I still felt unsatisfied with my trip to Las Vegas yet dreading to be back in the frustrating reality of taking care of my grandmother without appreciation. I was determined to perform my duty as the responsible grandson. It was difficult but I was able to rush back home to take care of my grandmother because my mom had to go to work, and my dad left for work at five o'clock in the morning. We arrived at seven o'clock in the morning. Upon my arrival, my partner Alvie and I saw my mom had just drove off to work. We drove through the night and quickly ate on the highway to make sure that we reached L.A. in time. I was drained from staying up late that I slept while he drove most of the way. Halfway through the drive we switched duties giving I'm time to rest. I found myself exhausted trying to live my life while taking care of my grandmother simultaneously.

As the years went on, her Alzheimer's and dementia progressed, and her condition got worse. Eventually, we had to put her in a hospital because she could no longer walk or feed herself with the help of anybody available, including myself. The situation went out of our control, and a part of me felt like I had failed. I felt futile as I wasn't able to give her the comfort and attention that she needed. It felt like I didn't take good enough care of her, so she ended up being admitted to the hospital again. I just took on that feeling of failure and held it tight. Even though that experience was challenging for me, I still tend to see the positive aspect of it. Due to this valuable life phase, I learned many essential life lessons and benefits.

One of these lessons was self-love. I cared for someone and saw them smile excitedly every day when they woke up, yet I stayed in an abusive relationship with Drew who was top of mind and made the conscious choice to disrespect me and intentionally hurt me. She helped me gather the courage to end things with him. She showed me that there's more to life than being with somebody who knows my name—knows who I am and who I'm supposed to be to them—and continues to disrespect me. She taught me such a valuable lesson that I will cherish forever. I learned patience, as caring for someone in her condition requires it.

Continuous repetitive instruction, convincing her to do daily tasks when she didn't want to. She also encouraged me to practice my Arabic because she could no longer speak English and could only communicate in her native language. I'm not sure how valuable this lesson was, but it allowed me to enjoy my heritage more than before. Lastly, appreciation. After all, we never know when will be the last time we are around them, see their smile, their laughs, even the frustrating moments that seem sweet to have. Her teachings and lessons will always remain etched in my mind. I felt grateful that I could spend the last few years with her, help her, and make her as comfortable as possible. I knew I was doing a good job at it.

During all those years, one thing really bruised me. I could never forget how my mom treated me when I asked her if she could give me a few more hours every two weeks since I was doing all the work. I didn't understand how she got so selfish. How could she use her son to make money? Moreover, what hurt was her response to that when she called me ungrateful and selfish and many other names simply because I requested fair compensation for doing 80 percent of the work while receiving only 20 percent of the income, despite the other person collecting 80 percent.

After my grandmother was admitted to the hospital, I was working part-time at a spin studio. As a spin instructor, that morning stands out in my memory. I had been sleeping in her room for easier access to the front door as she was in hospice care. At three o'clock, I woke up and felt like someone was watching me. It didn't feel malicious, just unfamiliar. I recall looking directly into a corner of her room above the door. While in her bedroom, I shockingly stared at that space for about 5 to 10 seconds. I was so scared and didn't understand what to do. So, I just immediately clenched my eyes and went back to sleep. Afterward, I woke up as usual and made it to work on time. Just as I was about to teach my first class of the day, I got a call from my dad. My heart skipped a beat as I answered the call. I remember all I heard from the other side was that my grandmother was no longer breathing. As soon as I was done with work, I rushed to the hospital. I got into her room and found that she was no longer alive. Her body was still warm, as it was only maybe an hour or so after she had just passed.

They were giving us time to say our goodbyes. What was bittersweet to hear was that I was told before she passed, she kept asking for "that boy," me. I felt torn hearing that she was yearning for me. Since she forgot my name, she kept asking where "that boy" was. I remember being sad, but at the same time, I also felt relieved that she was not living in a world where she couldn't operate in the way that she wanted to. Fast forward a few years, I had explored the idea of chatting with a medium to help me with getting closure to this experience. I gave her a photo and she filled in all of the blanks. She was spot on with what was happening during the situation I had asked her what happened the night I woke up. She had stated that it was my distant relative coming to get my grandmother. Which sounded eerie since that was the night before her passing. But this helped me close that experience in my mind. As much of a logical person I am, something in me said to reach for something that can't always be explained. Whether you are someone who believes in the supernatural or not, closure is always healthy. If that means you get an explanation to why something happened or to know that there is nothing to be explained. You move on.

After the funeral, I focused on my life and decided to get a full-time job to distance myself from my family, as I was feeling overwhelmed by their constant demands for help. It seemed like asking for favors from me had become a habit. Caring for someone for three years was a beautiful journey, but emotionally, it was draining. As I mentioned, I wasn't prepared for it and was forced to mature quickly.

I applied for a full-time job as a personal trainer at a new gym, where I quickly became one of the busiest trainers. This job helped me regain the energy I lost during the caretaking process and started my journey of physically disconnecting from my family to become more independent. However, my challenges did not stop there.

Chapter 5: The Good Employee

From a young age, we're taught to work hard and push ourselves to meet our expectations. But what happens when those lessons, rooted in our upbringing, carry the weight of unresolved childhood traumas? The values that our parents instill in us—values born out of their fears and experiences—can shape us in ways we don't fully understand until adulthood. For some, these lessons become a double-edged sword, leading to a work ethic that is both commendable and damaging. This revolves around the deep connections between childhood experiences and adult life, particularly in the workplace.

My journey to becoming a "good employee" began in the muted tones of my childhood home. My father, an inspiration of strong determination, often recounted his own immigrant story. Arriving in the United States at the tender age of twenty-seven, he possessed little more than a suitcase filled with dreams and a stubborn spirit. His narrative unfolded like a classic American tale. From the humble beginnings of sorting mail in a bustling post office to a successful rise to the position of a CPA, it was all the result of my father's hard work and determination. His story was a demonstration of the power of effort and perseverance.

His words resonated deeply within me and my brother. We witnessed firsthand the fruits of his labor: the comfortable home he had built and the security he provided for our family. His accomplishments were a tangible manifestation of the American Dream, a goal he instilled in us from a very young age. My father's relentless work ethic became a guiding principle in our lives. We were encouraged to strive for excellence in everything we did, to see challenges as opportunities for growth, and to never settle for mediocrity. His stories of late nights, early mornings, and countless hours spent studying were endless reminders of the sacrifices he had made to ensure our future. However, while my father's values were undoubtedly admirable, they also unintentionally created an unhealthy pressure to succeed. The expectation to be self-made and to achieve financial independence at a young age could be overwhelming. It often felt like there was no room for error or margin for mistakes.

The situation of my father's generation was vastly different from our own. The cost of living was significantly lower, and a modest income could provide a comfortable standard of living. However, the values he instilled in us stretched beyond financial success. One of the most lasting lessons I learned from my father was the importance of adaptation. He stressed the value of blending in to find common ground with colleagues and nurturing positive relationships within the workplace. He worked hard to integrate—grabbing weekly lunches with co-workers and networking—given that he essentially came from nothing. He believed that by refining a sense of belonging, I would create a more favorable environment for myself, thus increasing my chances of advancement. However, I struggled with becoming a "Yes Man." While I understood the value of maintaining a positive attitude and avoiding unnecessary conflicts, I also recognized the importance of critical thinking and self-advocacy. I soon found myself grappling with conflicting thoughts about what I was taught and what I was feeling.

My father's emphasis on conformity sometimes felt at odds with my desire to challenge the status quo and question authority. This internal conflict would later become apparent in my own professional experiences. As I navigated various work environments, I often found myself torn between the desire to please my superiors and the need to express my opinions and ideas. While well-intentioned, the legacy of my father's values sometimes made it difficult for me to strike the right balance. His emphasis on conformity extended beyond the workplace. He often advised me to avoid rocking the boat and to refrain from asking questions that might upset those in positions of authority. His experiences as an immigrant were tied to his desire to succeed in a foreign land, instilling in him a deep-seated fear of standing out negatively.

On the other hand, my mother had the advantage of arriving in the United States at a younger age, which allowed her to pursue higher education and gain a foothold in American society more easily. Despite her relative privilege, she still faced the challenges of cultural assimilation and the pressure to succeed as the eldest sibling in her family. My parents conveyed a message that resonated deeply with me and my brother: anything less than excellence was not worth pursuing. This applied to both our academic achievements and our future careers. They believed hard work and dedication were the keys to unlocking opportunities and achieving financial success.

The expectation to be the best and outperform our peers could sometimes be overwhelming. The underlying motivation behind my parents' emphasis on hard work was a desire to provide for their families. They came to the United States seeking better opportunities, driven by a deep responsibility to their loved ones. Their experiences had taught them that financial security was essential for building a stable and fulfilling life. For many immigrants, financial success is often seen as a tangible measure of achievement. My parents were no exception; they believed that hard work and dedication were the only ways to seize opportunities and provide a better life for their family.

Their emphasis on self-promotion was another important aspect of their values. They encouraged me to let my accomplishments be known and to highlight my skills and contributions. They had employed this strategy in their careers, believing self-promotion was essential for advancement while avoiding any less savory acts.

Though I strived to be successful in all areas of my life, my passion for learning did not ignite until much later. As a child, I found school to be a boring and often frustrating experience. The prospect of sitting down and memorizing facts for exams filled me with anxiety. My interests lay elsewhere, in activities that allowed me to be creative and explore my curiosity—interests my parents dismissed as mere extracurriculars. The constant comparisons and expectations to succeed made me feel insignificant and inadequate. It was a heavy burden, especially when I struggled to find my own path. While I could achieve good grades, my academic performance did not always align with my parents' expectations. The pressure to excel and be the best could be overwhelming, particularly when my natural inclinations lay more in the creative realm.

My parents' intense disappointment only strengthened my sense of inadequacy. Their belief that a strong work ethic was synonymous with academic achievement made it difficult for them to understand my struggles. My creative pursuits seemed to be viewed as distractions, departures from the path they had envisioned for me. However, my creative talents were a source of strength and comfort. Drawing, sketching, and exploring the world of art provided an outlet for my expression and allowed me to discover my unique voice.

In high school, I enhanced my artistic abilities by taking advanced art classes and immersing myself in the creative world. My success in this area gave me a sense of validation and accomplishment that I had often lacked in other aspects of my life. However, becoming a successful artist or working as a chef seemed less valuable—if not insignificant—compared to more traditional career paths. My parents struggled to envision a future where I could earn a comfortable living and achieve financial stability through creative pursuits, which was a significant source of disappointment for me as my passion in this field only grew.

Their constant discouragement deeply impacted my self-esteem and my willingness to pursue my dreams. I felt I was constantly fighting against their expectations, trying to prove that my artistic talents were valuable and worthy of pursuit. This internal conflict continued well into my adulthood. The pressure to prove myself to my parents and demonstrate that I could achieve success in a traditional career often overshadowed my desires and passions. It was a heavy burden, sometimes making it difficult to fully embrace my true self.

To survive, I adopted their beliefs about working hard, being a hustler, grinding, and keeping a very busy schedule when I could. I left no time to waste. When I turned 16, my dad got me my first job as a grocery bagger at Ralph's. He told me he had contacted a few people and made connections. When I submitted my application virtually, they would immediately interview and hire me on the spot. So, I went ahead and did that. As with any new habit a teenager learns, like getting a job for the first time, it was hard. I genuinely disliked going to work. I would call out often because I wasn't enjoying it, and it wasn't fun, not to mention my problematic manager.

The demands of my academic and athletic pursuits compounded the challenges I faced in the workplace. Balancing my studies, sports practices, and part-time work at the grocery store was a constant juggling act. When I confided in my father about the difficulties I was experiencing with my manager, he quickly intervened. His connections and influence within the company led to the transfer of the problematic manager, demonstrating his unwavering support for my well-being and success. However, despite this positive outcome, I still disliked the job and remained in it for a total of four months. The experience, while challenging, provided valuable lessons in responsibility and time management.

As I stated earlier, I had to juggle work, academia, and sports. My parents' views on sports were bluntly different from mine. While they recognized the importance of physical activity, they did not prioritize athletics like I did. They saw sports as a recreational activity—a way to stay healthy and have fun. However, I believed that my athletic achievements could open doors for me and provide scholarships and college admission opportunities. This difference in perspective often led to conflicts and misunderstandings. My parents' insistence on prioritizing academics and work over athletics was frustrating and disheartening.

The constant pressure to balance work, school, and sports could be overwhelming. However, I was determined to prove myself and demonstrate that I could excel in all areas of my life. I pushed through the stress, maintained my focus, and continued striving for excellence in my academic and athletic endeavors. My transition to a retail job significantly shifted my career trajectory. While the corporate aspect of the role was still present, I found the work more engaging and fulfilling. I enjoyed interacting with customers and using my creativity to enhance the shopping experience. However, the demands of my job also meant that I missed out on many typical experiences that teenagers enjoy. The constant pressure to work and excel limited my opportunities for socializing, pursuing hobbies, and simply enjoying my youth.

An incident with an award ceremony was a particularly painful reminder of the sacrifices I had made to balance my work and athletic commitments. Despite my efforts to plan ahead and secure a day off, I was ultimately denied the opportunity to attend this significant event. The manager's decision felt like a cruel joke, disregarding my priorities, despite ample notice and the importance of this occasion. During my shift that day, my manager had said I could take my lunch and drive to my award ceremony since it was my senior year of high school. I got to my school just as the award ceremony concluded. The news that I had received the "Most Valuable Player" award, delivered by my peers, was a bittersweet victory. While I was honored and grateful for the recognition, I couldn't help but feel a pang of regret for not having advocated for myself more to be there. But the fear of making my manager angry or disappointing my parents for missing work won out. Celebrating my achievements with my teammates and coaches was a missed opportunity that I would never get back. This was a lesson in the importance of advocating for oneself and setting clear boundaries, even when faced with resistance. As a creative person, I didn't often go outside and get dirty, and I worked hard to change my image in high school to become a successful person that my parents could be proud of. The pressure to meet my parents' expectations and the demands of my academic and athletic pursuits had taken a toll on my well-being. Along with making my parents proud, I found myself also seeking affirmation from my peers. As a gay teen not yet out, I wanted to physically change my image and adopted a very unhealthy lifestyle. As if my desire to be the best for my parents wasn't enough, I wanted to be the best socially. Desperate to look like the guy girls wished they dated and the guy all the guys wanted to be friends with, I spiraled into unhealthy eating habits, anorexia, overtraining, and neglecting my very average GPA.

Despite recognizing the negative impact of this stress, I found it difficult to let go of the desire for their approval. Watching my brother's struggles, while different from mine, provided a blunt contrast. His inability to maintain a consistent work ethic and manage his finances highlighted the importance of personal responsibility and self-discipline, which I wanted to demonstrate I had.

As I transitioned to college, sports became more of a recreational outlet. The gym provided a much-needed escape from the stress and pressures of my life. However, my relentless pursuit of physical perfection and financial success remained a driving force. I found myself grasping for any job opportunity that would increase my earnings. The desire to provide for myself and my family had become a deeply rooted part of my identity. The transient nature of my early jobs was a constant source of frustration. The temporary nature of these positions meant that I was constantly searching for new opportunities, which could be both time-consuming and stressful. I ended up bouncing from one job to the next every four to six months. Though I had no issues getting a job, I longed for something more permanent. It started to feel like when I would tell my parents I was heading to work or tried to pick up an extra shift, they seemed unimpressed with how hard I was working because working in retail was not a viable long-term career. So I started researching how to make those roles more permanent, trying to work my way up to a keyholder or manager. Those titles started to give me hope.

Despite the challenges, I remained focused on financial advancement. With its slightly higher hourly rate, each new job represented a step forward in my career. I shared these accomplishments with my father while seeking his approval and validation. However, my father's perspective on work-life balance was far from ideal.

Any time I spent socializing, pursuing hobbies, or engaging in self-care was seen as a waste of time. His firm belief in the primacy of work often overshadowed the importance of rest, relaxation, and personal well-being. Hanging out with friends looked more like wasting money than mental well-being; buying new clothes or things I felt I earned was a waste when I could be at home or being productive to save money. Everything outside of home or work was considered a waste of time or money rather than life-enhancing experiences or momentary joys. As I continued my education at a junior college, I faced additional challenges due to the school's seniority system. The limited availability of certain courses made it difficult to progress through my degree program, which led to extreme frustration and anxiety. Because I was struggling to get the courses I needed, at one point, I contemplated dropping out of college and just focusing on working full-time. While I was working, I wasn't making a lot of money. With that said, I was also applying for multiple credit cards, and at that point, I had gotten myself into so much credit card debt as a 23-year-old that I felt like I was drowning and couldn't even pay those minimum balances. I knew if my parents found out about it, I would be done for.

The constant pressure to succeed and meet expectations could be overwhelming, leading me to contemplate dropping out of college. However, my mother's surprising support for an online accelerated program gave me hope. Her encouragement allowed me to balance my education with my work commitments, ensuring I could continue earning a living while pursuing my degree. This was a significant turning point in my life, as it demonstrated that my parents' values were not entirely rigid and were willing to support my choices, even if they deviated from their expectations. I graduated from college with a fresh sense of confidence and took the leap to apply for a full-time position as a personal trainer. The fitness industry was a natural fit, combining my passion for health and wellness with my desire to help others. As I shared each phase of the process with my parents, they still needed convincing that I could make this a full-time, successful career rather than a hobby. With every phase, I explained the job in great detail, using buzzwords I knew my dad would approve of, like "This job gives me health benefits!" and "This job offers bonuses for success," making sure to paint a picture of success and viability for my parents.

Surprisingly, I secured the position and was a top-performing trainer within two weeks of the gym's opening. This achievement marked a significant milestone in my career, demonstrating the skills and experience I had gained through my years of hard work and dedication. Furthermore, my grandmother's passing was a catalyst for personal growth and transformation. It was a time of reflection and introspection during which I realized it was time to take control of my life and pursue my passions. What was most jarring about that experience was when I shared news of my financial success with my dad upon receiving my first paycheck. For context, this two-week paycheck was more than what I made in past jobs over a three-month period. He responded with "Good" in a very content tone and then immediately asked me if he could borrow money to pay off some doctor's bills. I immediately interrogated him as he had asked for $1000. I found out he needed less than requested wanting extra just in case he forgot about something. The disappointment, anger, and confusion I experienced were consuming me. This incident marked a turning point in our relationship; it wasn't that my love for him changed, but I now felt like I was becoming my father's caregiver, questioning why he needed my money and why he did not seem to have any for his expenses when he clearly made more than me. It forced me to reassess the dynamics between us and realize I was no longer the child seeking approval. Instead, I was becoming the adult, the provider, the source of support he was starting to need.

Despite my financial struggles, the expectation that I would be willing to lend my parents money, or that they started telling me I had to start paying for certain things in the home, revealed a deep-seated belief that their needs always came first and my personal responsibilities had to take a back seat. It was a reminder of the power imbalances that can exist within family relationships, even when the roles shift. My mother's scolding phone call at 8:00 p.m. while I was working further indicated her continued expectations. Despite my long hours and dedication to my work, she seemed unable to comprehend the demands of my profession. It was a frustrating reminder of the generational differences and the challenges of navigating never-ending family dynamics.

Moreover, my mother's doubt about my late-night work hours further indicated her struggle to understand the demands of my profession. Her disbelief highlighted the generational differences and the challenges of adapting to a rapidly changing workplace. Despite my efforts to explain my work commitments, my parents questioned my dedication and commitment. Their perception of my work ethic was shaped by their own experiences, which were often rooted in more traditional and predictable work environments. However, my financial success was undeniable. The increased income I brought home each month was a tangible demonstration of my hard work and dedication. It was a source of pride for me and a way to prove to my parents that my career choices were valid and worthwhile.

Another significant milestone was the opportunity to secure my own apartment. It represented a brand-new sense of independence and autonomy that allowed me to create my own space and establish my own routines. As I tried to show my mom my newly earned space, she pursed her lips in disenchantment and said the apartment looked "alright," making unimpressed facial expressions and shrugging her shoulders. It was a blow to my ego that my hard work and dedication could afford me my own space, and yet it was not good enough for her because now it was considered a waste of my money. A few months after that incident with my mom, I received a notice that I would be promoted from trainer to Fitness Manager. It was something I had set as a goal from the beginning of my hire, and a couple of my coworkers got promoted before me, which made it that much more desirable. My promotion to management would further validate my skills and abilities and was a testament to the hard work and dedication I had invested in my career. However, it also brought with it new challenges and responsibilities. I made sure to seek advice from a successful manager in the company at a high-volume location, which was a proactive step in ensuring my continued success—or so I thought. Learning from the experiences of others is a valuable strategy for career development. I contacted this manager and asked if he could help me better understand the role I would be undertaking and how to be successful in that position. The encounter with my colleague was not what I had anticipated. What was supposed to be a productive night of collaboration and personal development turned into something a bit more sinister. While we were conversing over some food, it seemed harmless as we only spoke about our careers and what I needed to learn, along with some shop talk. After dinner, he encouraged me to attend a local gay bar with him. The night was young, and I figured it would be a great bonding experience. For context, he worked in West Hollywood, and we had dinner at his workplace. After only a drink, I stated that it was time to go since we both had an early workday the following morning. He said he felt very tipsy, and I did not feel comfortable having him drive home, especially since he was wearing a brace on his dominant foot. So, using the accelerator with a braced foot while being intoxicated added more of a challenge. Knowing his drive was on my way home, I suggested that I could take him home. He quickly accepted my offer.

Upon exiting the parking garage of the gym where his car was, he asked me to stop the car in an urgent tone. Panicked, I stopped and asked questions to make sure he was alright. He then said in an assertive tone, “Kiss me!” I needed a second to collect my thoughts. I wasn’t expecting that. I further interrogated him, asking what sparked that statement since he was married to a woman and had three children. He responded with, "When I first met you, I thought you were the most beautiful thing." Stunned and moderately uncomfortable, I kept driving. He started making sexual advances on me as I was driving him home. A part of me thought, "Maybe I need to play this game to get ahead." I almost acted on that thought, knowing how much authority he commanded within the company. It could potentially solidify my success, but it would also be my ruin. Remember, I was desperate to prove to my family I could make a career out of fitness. I rejected him and reminded him that he had a wife and three children to consider and if he was working on self-discovery. I gladly offered to be an outlet, but I was not in the business of sleeping with a colleague, let alone breaking up a family. Days later, he continued to pursue me in a romantic way. His inappropriate advances, fueled by a sense of entitlement, were a violation of my boundaries and a deeply disturbing experience.

Therefore, maintaining professionalism and rejecting his advances was a difficult decision, but it was the right one. I knew that compromising my values and allowing myself to be manipulated would have long-lasting consequences. I shared my experience with my roommate, who provided me with much-needed support and guidance. She helped me navigate the complexities of the situation by offering advice on how to move forward and protect myself. This incident highlighted the power imbalances that can exist within the workplace. My roommate's advice to maintain a professional relationship with my colleague was essential.

Despite the challenges, I managed to navigate the situation without compromising my integrity or jeopardizing my job. However, the consequences of my actions were far-reaching, and I would later learn how toxic my workplace could become.

During the first few months of my promotion, I was transferred to two separate locations. The decision to relocate to a new apartment significantly disrupted my life. The transition to a new living situation was stressful and time-consuming, but I was moving to my dream location—a high-volume club—which was my initial goal. It quickly became a bittersweet experience. While it represented a professional achievement, it also meant working alongside the same manager who had made inappropriate advances. The transition to this new location was ironic; on the one hand, it presented exciting opportunities for career growth. On the other hand, it forced me to confront the ongoing challenges and toxic dynamics within the workplace. What I would soon realize would be my worst nightmare. The transition from one living situation to another was one headache, but then transferring to a location where I had to work with the manager who had made a sexual pass at me made it even harder. The aftertaste of that experience was still palpable. We had to work in the same office, and we would have periodic meetings. I tried very hard to remain as professional as possible, not allowing him to speak negatively of me. But that didn't stop him from fabricating situations to our higher-ups.

My father's advice to "grin and bear it" echoed in my mind, reminding me of the importance of avoiding conflict and maintaining a positive image. However, this internal conflict made it difficult for me to speak out against the injustices I was experiencing. The surprise attack meeting with my superiors was a devastating blow. The accusations leveled against me were baseless and hurtful. My superiors stated that I was being inappropriate with members on the gym floor along with other accusations of malpractice. It was painful to see the power dynamics at play in the workplace and the potential for retaliation. The betrayal of my colleagues, who had failed to provide me with the necessary feedback, added to my frustration and disappointment.

The situation was an intricate web of manipulation and deceit that left me feeling powerless and alone. Sharing this experience with my parents would have undoubtedly led to a familiar response and strengthened their argument that I would never be able to make fitness a career. Their emphasis on avoiding conflict and maintaining a positive image would likely have prevented me from seeking justice or addressing the toxic situation. I knew they would ask me what I did wrong to cause that situation. Again, in their eyes, I may have said something to make somebody angry or done something to make someone think twice about me working at that location. It was never the job's fault; it was always the employee's fault.

After being transferred to a new location and spending only three months in my managerial position there, I was unexpectedly asked to leave my high-paying job. The regional manager, who stated that I was one of the most honest managers he had worked with, asked me to step down from my position because my "maturation" was not where it needed to be. In a shaky voice, fearful of advocating for myself, I asked, "How can my maturation not be where you need it to be when you have moved me frequently, and yet I am hitting goals at this location?" It was an honest question to which he had no reasonable explanation. I was told my salary would conclude in three days and that I could either stay with the company as a trainer or voluntarily leave. Desperate to stay financially stable and not embarrass myself, I stayed, leaving me frantic and uncertain about my future.

Desperate for a solution, I vented to my parents that I was more afraid of being broke and losing all I had worked hard for than I was of their approval. My mom suggested I look into teaching. It was not the career path I had anticipated, but I needed the stability. I took my mom's suggestion to become a teacher, not only to gain some financial stability but also in the hope of appeasing my parents, as I had just told them I had failed at making my passion for fitness a career. I had always prioritized their approval over my passions, which didn't align with teaching. However, I went through the motions to earn their praise and respect. I could see my mom light up with joy when she talked shop with me about teaching lesson planning. It also provided her with a chauffeur to district meetings, during which she would complain about having to drive herself or go with her sister.

This was a stable job—one of the pillars of my dad's lessons about getting a stable job. The other pillar was to ensure you had health insurance and benefits. The last pillar was to secure a 401(k) plan or some sort of pension to set yourself up for the future. As an immigrant, he struggled for many of these things and only wanted to ensure my security for the long run, even if that meant shelving my passions. Even then, my parents still felt I was taking my passion a little too seriously.

As a teacher, I felt unfulfilled, stuck in a classroom teaching from a textbook to disinterested high school students, though there were some moments of joy. I received praise from strangers who discovered I was an educator, and I had control over my classroom—something I felt I lacked while working for a major corporation like Equinox. My passion lay elsewhere—in personal training, where I was helping clients become healthier versions of themselves. Aside from the typical issues I faced in a gym setting, people wanted to be there. To cope, I sought ways to supplement my income outside of teaching by doing what I loved, even if it wasn't in a gym. Over four years, I grew into my teaching role and discovered I was a skilled educator, impacting many students' lives. Though I loved teaching people I never thought that I was a great teacher or leader. It was a dream of mine to get to a position to lead people at work, but I did not think I was prepared when the offer was given. As a manager at a luxury gym I enjoyed sharing my perspective, skill and knowledge on what I was educating my team and clients I would train, seeing them succeed from that information made me feel amazing. This was the same with teaching high school students. My students often complimented that I was one of only a few teachers they have ever had that would truly lecture and engage with them over assigning work without context, making their time in my class enjoyable. Through that I gained the respect of all of my students, yet a sense of emptiness lingered.

While I was dating Jon, who came into my life during my transition into teaching, he noticed my financial challenges. At first, it wasn't too much of an issue, but as our time together grew, he started to feel that I wasn't able to make enough money compared to him. I was already feeling stressed from taking a pay cut, but now I was feeling pressure from my partner. It felt similar to living at home and wanting to prove myself to my parents. As time progressed, the tension grew more intense, causing me to eventually get a second job as a group fitness instructor. Though he seemed supportive, I found myself still seeking further approval that I was good enough. This made work rapidly unenjoyable when he wouldn't show the slightest interest in my successes and then complained that he wished I could do more around the house. It completely changed the dynamic of our relationship. Eventually, my body could not take the second job, as it was physically taxing, so along with ending that relationship, I left that job and moved back home.

Another area that added stress was the constant ridicule and frustration my parents directed at me for periodically moving out and back into their home. As soon as I left, they put my room to use for themselves. Once I finally told them I was moving home to save money, they immediately started hounding me about how I made poor choices in life. This was a recurring theme anytime I wanted to do something they did not value or perceived as a monumental decision. While rebuilding my self-esteem at their home, I found myself prepping for a bodybuilding competition that kept me hyper-focused on myself and my responsibilities. That competition changed how I saw fitness for the better and further proved my point that fitness can be a successful career.

Eventually, the world went into chaos as the novel COVID virus spread. While things were closed and people were separated, I found myself thriving during that time. I noticed that people were still focused on being physically healthy, even with commercial gyms closed due to the pandemic. Moving back home to save money, I had an epiphany: to build a gym in my backyard. This spark of inspiration would change everything. While teaching virtually during the pandemic, I found myself redefining what it meant to be a hard worker and a good employee. With newfound free time before classes and early dismissal times, I reignited my passion for personal training, taking on private clients from my home. This supplemental income and passion project allowed me to rediscover my entrepreneurial spirit, which had been dormant since my parents discouraged me from pursuing fitness full-time. My parents noticed my success and entrepreneurial drive as I continued teaching and training clients. They proudly showcased my home gym to visiting guests, and I started sharing my workouts on social media, gaining traction and connecting with others during a time when we were all craving human interaction. Through this journey, I slowly rebuilt my confidence and redefined my dad's lessons, realizing that being a good employee meant more than just stability and benefits. I learned to prioritize my passions and creativity, laying the groundwork for a new chapter in my life. In mid-2021, an unexpected opportunity arose, setting me on a path of self-discovery and transformation. Thanks to the lessons I learned during the pandemic and the rediscovery of my entrepreneurial spirit, I was finally ready to embark on a journey that would align my passions, values, and career, but it also thrust me into change, which I was unprepared for.

Chapter 6: What Did It Cost?

As I continued my career in education, I realized that there was a sense of fulfillment that came with helping others grow and learn. Each day brought new challenges, and while I enjoyed the work, a subtle but persistent feeling lingered—a void I couldn't quite place at first. Despite my professional contentment, something felt incomplete. I realized what I was missing only when I turned my attention inward: it was my passion for fitness. Though I was training part-time, I was starting to feel burnt out. I was burning the candle at both ends. I needed something to help recharge my battery and infuse more joy into my life. So, I started dating again. But we won't get too deep into that.

Fitness had always been an important part of my life, but in the hustle of building a career, I had let it slip into the background. Now, I knew it was time to reclaim that part of myself—not just as a hobby but as a way to enrich my life. I had always said to myself and others that if a career opportunity came along where fitness would be my sole focus, along with making enough money to sustain a comfortable living, I would jump at the chance.

During the pandemic, I found the perfect outlet to fill that void—working independently in fitness. It brought a sense of happiness and fulfillment that I hadn't experienced in a long time. However, this newfound joy was tempered by my growing frustration as a teacher in Los Angeles. In my sector, teachers weren't paid during the summer months, leaving me in a constant scramble to find ways to supplement my income. I often found myself working full-time hours—or even more—just to get by during what was supposed to be a fun summer break. This cycle of uncertainty only deepened my desire to pursue something more stable and personally fulfilling. Though I had someone in my life who helped distract me from my negative feelings, he could only do so much, as the reality was that I was not making close to the income I earned during my working months.

I was working around 60 hours a week, juggling my responsibilities as a teacher and my commitments to fitness clients, all in an effort to save enough to ease the financial strain during the unpaid summer months. Thankfully, we were teaching from a distance as the fear of COVID lingered throughout the world, so I saved at least some money on gas. The goal was to maintain a higher income for two and a half to three months, which would allow me to return to my regular teaching schedule once the summer ended. Luckily, I was living at home due to the pandemic, so my basic overhead costs were low. When the impact of COVID started to subside, schools reopened, and I was back on campus, content with my decision to continue teaching. It was a noble job; I had a pension and a stable income through the school year, and it allowed my parents to stop worrying about me while still enabling me to pursue fitness. However, deep down, I was still yearning for something more that could push me further and reward me financially for my efforts. I felt I deserved more. I was more than just a school teacher or a part-time fitness professional. I'm a highly educated, enthusiastic person who not only loves fitness but lives the model lifestyle we see on social media today. To mask my negative feelings, I periodically accepted invitations to do photoshoots, but only in secret, since my parents did not approve of displaying my physique for photos, even if it was done artistically or to help push my career forward.

One afternoon, while prepping my students for their final exams, an email landed in my inbox. It was from a recruiter who had come across my social media presence and thought I'd be a great fit for a role at their fitness company. Not having heard of the company before, I Googled it to see what product they were promoting. Coincidentally, as the pandemic started, I had received ads for an at-home strength training device that could track your movement, count your reps, and perform other functions that trainers typically do. Having had less-than-ideal experiences with fitness companies in the past, I didn't think much of it. I responded calmly, acknowledging their interest and agreeing to a phone interview. The phone interview was nothing out of the ordinary—just a series of typical questions. A few days later, I received another email. This time, the company wanted to schedule an official virtual interview. Although we were still navigating the restrictions of the pandemic, they aimed to make the interview process as close to a traditional in-person experience as possible.

At that moment, I began to realize that this opportunity could be a turning point—one that might finally allow me to explore a career beyond my current boundaries. After about

30 to 40 minutes of conversation, the interview felt great. However, I didn't dwell on it too much, assuming they might choose someone they felt was more qualified or—like other companies—offer lower income for more work. Then, to my surprise, I received another email requesting a second interview, this time with their head of education. I completed that interview successfully and moved on to the next stage, which involved more formal interviews with different members of the staff and the team I could potentially be working with. Since the semester had ended and summer had begun, I was willing to invest time in attending these virtual interviews. By this time, I had met with eight different people and shared my experience with my partner and parents. My dad scoffed and said, "Well, don't jeopardize your job for something that hasn't happened yet." However, my partner's unwavering support countered the negativity of that statement.

As the process advanced, they informed me that the next step was a screen test—essentially, an audition—since this was a virtual fitness company. They needed to ensure that I looked good on paper and had the presence and delivery required to connect with their audience on camera. I was so excited by this opportunity that I eagerly arranged a flight to San Francisco for the audition. They generously offered to cover the cost of my flight and hotel stay, so I just needed to be there from Friday to Sunday, with my screen test scheduled for Saturday. I was beyond excited. I told my family and shared the news with my parents—it was something I never anticipated happening. The opportunity to pursue my passion for fitness had unexpectedly landed in my lap. The excitement was overwhelming.

When I arrived in San Francisco, they booked me into a beautiful hotel that was far more luxurious than I was used to. They instructed me to submit all receipts for compensation, including flight and hotel expenses. It was all very surreal. Before the screen test, they sent me a workout to prepare—a 20-minute routine that I had to study and plan to demonstrate my knowledge on camera. As a perfectionist, I was determined to absolutely nail this audition. I wanted to leave no room for doubt.

On the day of the audition, I was met by two women: one was an assistant to the coaches, and the other was a technician. This was my moment to shine, and I was fully prepared to give it everything I had. I entered a black, soundproofed room with a full rig filled with lights, cameras at three different angles, and a mat, which was my mark. They introduced me to the equipment and the weights. They also gave me a rundown of the cameras' positions and how the timer would work. While standing in that room, I felt nervous. It felt like this could be my one chance to leave teaching behind and fully follow my passion for fitness.

As the test began, things started off fairly well, though I was nervous and shaky. In the middle of a transition between exercises, I noticed the weights were a bit more worn than I expected. I could manage, but switching them on and off the bar wasn't as easy as I would have liked. I tried to stay composed and decided not to change the weight after a quick failed attempt. With the same weight that I had been squatting with, I swiftly transitioned to an overhead press. If you know basic muscle groups, you'll understand that moving from a leg-based squat to pressing a heavy weight over your head isn't ideal at the same weight. My arms were struggling, but I kept a big smile on my face and ran purely on adrenaline. I was determined not to stop, even though it was challenging.

When the 20-minute workout was over, I immediately asked, “How did I do?” patiently awaiting feedback. They responded positively and told me that it was great. Nervously, I asked if they needed another take, but they reassured me, “No, you did fantastically.” Hearing those words made all the nerves and effort worth it. After hearing the feedback, "We could really see your excitement doing what you love," it hit me—I had done it. I returned to my hotel room and shared the news with my partner, who was just as thrilled. However, there was a possibility that they might need me to return for a follow-up on Sunday, so I stayed an extra day while anxiously awaiting further instructions, which thankfully did not come to pass.

Once I returned home, with summer vacation in full swing, I patiently awaited an email for their next steps. To my surprise, I didn’t hear anything from the company. I carried on with my routine: personal training clients when I could, working out, and spending time with my partner at the time. But the silence from the company started to weigh on me. Days turned into a week, one week turned into two, then two and a half, and eventually three weeks passed with no word.

I grew increasingly nervous and anxious since I was unaware if they had gone in a different direction, if I had made a mistake, or if they had decided not to hire anyone after all. The uncertainty troubled me. Eventually, I reached out to the person who had initially interviewed me and explained my situation. As a teacher, they begin assigning students to your classes mid-summer, so I needed to know whether to plan for the upcoming school year or move forward with this new chapter in fitness. The waiting was unbearable, and I needed clarity on what was next. I gently bumped her via email, letting her know I needed a decision soon. I explained that if they were offering me the position, I'd need to start the process of leaving the school district. However, if they weren't, I had to commit to returning to my teaching job. I immediately received a response saying we needed to schedule final interviews with the founders of the company. It seemed unusual to have this many interviews, but I happily obliged. I was pretty confident that the founders would like me and had what I considered a talent for interviewing. In fact, I had interviewed for and received almost every job I had applied for. I would say it's because I can read people really well and can anticipate what they want to hear. Over my years growing up in a home where all I wanted to do was please, I developed the ability to learn patterns and anticipate actions, desires, and potential emotional outcomes of people. Though this personality trait has its drawbacks, like setting boundaries, it comes in handy in professional settings to garner respect.

I managed to interview both of them within the same week and received rave reviews of my interviews afterward. By the following Friday, July 2nd, I was officially offered a full-time position with the online fitness company. I was thrilled—but there was one major caveat: I had to relocate to San Francisco. While I had imagined this possibility, the reality of moving hit me harder than I expected. I wasn't as ready as I thought I'd be.

As I discussed the offer on the phone, my mom sat off to the side and listened intently to the entire conversation. When I accepted the position, she heard it all. I turned to her and let her know that I had made my decision, though she already knew. She shrugged her shoulders and said, "Well, I guess you're leaving." It truly felt like a once-in-a-lifetime opportunity—something I might never get the chance to experience again. With that, I began planning the next chapter of my life. Excitedly, I secured an apartment within three weeks of the news and started preparing for the big move. The excitement was palpable; I was leaving my teaching career behind and embarking on a new journey. It felt like a peak moment in my life, but I wasn't quite prepared for everything that this new chapter would bring.

It was overwhelmingly exciting yet terrifying at the same time. Moving 350 miles away meant ending the relationship with the person I had been seeing in Los Angeles, which, at the time, felt like the right decision. I was riding high, feeling invincible, as though I couldn't make any wrong decisions. Each step I took seemed like the best one, and I was convinced that everything was falling perfectly into place; even my parents started to seem excited about this new chapter. Looking back, I realized that while many of my choices were sound, I may have rushed into some of them. I was eager to fill the void I had been feeling for so long, so I pushed forward quickly without considering the long-term consequences.

Nevertheless, I moved to San Francisco to set up my new apartment and began settling in. One thing that stood out during this time was something Kris had mentioned. She explained that my role would be a bit different from the other coaches since I was a strength coach. Most other coaches specialized in general fitness, HIIT, or boxing, so I wouldn't be integrated into the group in that way, I assumed. Instead, I'd be working more independently with a different manager. It struck me as a little odd, but I accepted it, trusting the process. Though everything seemed to be coming together, I soon learned that this interval would reveal itself in ways I hadn't predicted.

I wasn't about to question the hand that had just served me the biggest opportunity of my fitness career. So, I went along with it for the first couple of months, fully embracing my new role. I was writing workouts and planning recording sessions; everything felt perfect. I had so much free time that, for the first time, I was still being paid for working a full-time job while only clocking about 15 hours a week. The shift was drastic compared to my old life. I had been used to working 12-hour days, hustling between jobs, often sacrificing weekends for extra work. Now, I found myself working maybe two to three hours a day at my own pace, and I was earning double, if not triple, what I had made as a high school teacher. It felt almost dreamlike. I kept thinking, it can't get any better than this.

However, there was a challenge. Despite the success I was experiencing in my career, I didn't have any real connections in San Francisco. In Los Angeles, my social circle was made up of friends who helped shape my values, as well as my family—my mom and dad—who were always there to ground me and remind me of what was truly important, even if we had differing viewpoints. Now, I had stepped away from all of that. I was, in fact, alone; without a frame of reference, I had to create my own value system without their advice, opinions, or support. It was all on me. I thought I knew it all because I had an inflated ego from my success in LA. I was too confident, having garnered a lot of praise in LA for my hard work as well as my hard-earned physique.

I was determined not to fail at leaving my life in Los Angeles behind and building a community for myself. As I began searching for new connections in San Francisco, the challenge was far from how it felt. As a gay man living in an extremely liberal city in my thirties, I faced a whole new set of experiences and challenges that I hadn't encountered in Los Angeles. How could I? I was a highly sheltered person living in the bubble of Los Angeles, and though I had stints moving into my own apartments, I still had access to what was familiar and safe for me. This was completely different. I did not have the access to my support system like I did when I lived in Los Angeles. I was completely alone.

It was eye-opening and overwhelming to navigate this new environment while trying to establish a sense of belonging. San Francisco is where my anxiety really began to take root. I finally had the chance to meet the entire team in person, but it was an awkward experience from the start. My coworkers had been instructed not to communicate with me, and I was told the same—I couldn't really engage with them or work with them yet. To make matters worse, we had to stand in front of a camera and act as if we'd been friends for years. It was one of the most uncomfortable experiences I've ever had working for a brand or company. But I was able to grin and bear it through my learned behaviors.

Despite the initial awkwardness, we managed to get through it, and on the surface, it seemed like we all blended well. Everyone welcomed me with open arms, and I thought I'd finally have the chance to develop strong friendships and relationships with my colleagues. As someone who expresses care through acts of service and quality time—whether cooking for others or setting up an inviting space—I decided to throw a little housewarming party at my apartment. I let all my coworkers know about it and even sent out a Google form to get RSVPs, check for any food allergies, and see if anyone wanted to contribute something to the gathering.

Unfortunately, nobody from the team RSVP'd, and with no one attending, I ended up canceling the event. It was disheartening and left me feeling even more isolated. It took me back to when I turned 30 and invited many people to my birthday party, which I had invested time and money in to be a big event, but most of those I invited did not show up. I refused to let it consume me. I kept a happy demeanor at work and remained focused on building my community outside of it. During this time, I stayed in regular contact with my parents. Naturally, they were a bit saddened that I was no longer in Los Angeles, but that sadness quickly turned into frustration as my dad's health started to fluctuate. He was in and out of the hospital, and each time, my mom would call me frantic. She often made me feel guilty for leaving, saying things like, "I can't believe you've left me to handle this all by myself," as if my decision to move had somehow worsened my dad's condition or solidified that I abandoned her for good.

These conversations stirred up a lot of stress and unresolved trauma from my childhood. I hoped that the distance would change our dynamic for the better. I tried to brush it off and go about my day, but the guilt remained. I couldn't shake the feeling that I had abandoned my parents, much like my brother had when he joined the military and later moved out of state. It was a heavy emotional burden that I carried with me, even as I tried to navigate my new life in San Francisco. I attempted to distract myself from the constant guilt and stress by filling my time with work and trying to make social plans. However, no matter how much I immersed myself in these activities, I always ended up on the phone with my mom, listening to what issues awaited me back at home. Each conversation seemed to circle back to the same point—her making me feel guilty for leaving and for not being there to help with my dad's health issues. It felt like a never-ending cycle of emotional burden, and no matter what I did, I couldn't escape it. Phone calls ended in abrupt hang-ups or attempts to quickly get one another off the phone in the heat of a spat.

Adding to this frustration was the fact that, despite my efforts, I still hadn't made any solid friendships or romantic connections in San Francisco. I had been using a gay social app to meet other people in the city while hoping to build new relationships. Still, it quickly became apparent that most of the people I met were only interested in one thing—my body. They didn't care about my intelligence, my personality, or my desire for platonic companionship. This was the complete opposite of what I thought I would find in the city.

There were times when I felt the excitement of being newly single and in a new city, and I would go along with it, trying not to overthink and be open to whatever life gave me. I didn't want to hold myself back from new experiences, and part of me thought these encounters might eventually lead to something more meaningful. Over time, it became clear that this wasn’t the case. These superficial connections started to weigh heavily on me, making it almost impossible to build the deep, meaningful relationships I longed for, whether in a platonic or romantic sense. Each encounter left me feeling more disconnected and alone, reinforcing the isolation I already struggled with in this new chapter of my life.

One night, it felt like my entire world was crashing. By this point, I had been living in San Francisco for about six months and invited a friend—someone I was still getting to know—to stay the night. He lived across town and was not available until the evening; I didn't want to send him home after our hangout. So, I said, "Why don’t you come over? We can hang out, and you can stay over, but I have to be up early at 5 a.m. tomorrow, so please try not to arrive too late."

Despite my request, he didn’t show up until 10:30 p.m. By that time, I was already frustrated. I had gotten ready for bed, mentally prepared for the early morning ahead, and now I had lost an hour and a half of precious sleep. To put into context what work was the following day, I was to teach three hours of live fitness classes. My call time was at 6 a.m., and my on-camera time was promptly at 7 a.m. Still, I let him in, and we started chatting. I reminded him that I needed to be up early and would have to go to bed soon. We ended up lying in bed next to each other, and despite my exhaustion, things started to turn romantic. Being single and still exploring relationships in the city, I wasn’t against the idea of letting things develop. Yet, deep down, I knew this wasn’t what I needed at the moment. The whole situation, with its mix of frustration and fleeting connection, added to the emotional whirlwind that I was already experiencing.

Unfortunately, the situation quickly spiraled as I started to experience what I later realized was an anxiety attack. At the time, I just felt off. I asked my friend if we could just go to sleep, but as I lay there, I found myself tossing and turning, unable to get comfortable. My mind was racing with a flurry of thoughts, and I couldn't seem to shut it off.

I thought that maybe getting up to grab a glass of water would help, so I went to the kitchen, drank some water, and returned to bed. I was hoping it would ease whatever was going on. But the discomfort persisted. I had my weed pen with me, and since marijuana is legal in California, I took a couple of hits, thinking it might help me relax. Yet nothing seemed to work. My friend could tell something was wrong as I kept shifting in bed. He turned to me and asked if everything was okay, and I admitted that I didn't know. I told him I felt extremely off, my mind was racing, and I couldn't relax or fall asleep. Eventually, I decided it would be best if he left so I could be alone and still feel unsettled at midnight. In a desperate attempt to calm myself down, I grabbed my phone and started Googling my symptoms—an all-too-common mistake when anxiety takes hold. If you've ever experienced an anxiety attack, you know that self-diagnosing through Google is probably the worst thing you can do. Despite trying to wind myself down, nothing worked, and I was left alone with my thoughts that were struggling to regain control.

Eventually, I decided it was in my best interest to call the paramedics in case something was seriously wrong. By this point, it was 3:00 a.m., and I hesitated—feeling apologetic even as I dialed the number. It's so typical of me—apologizing for being a burden. It was a lesson that was ingrained in me by my parents, who always emphasized not inconveniencing others with personal problems. As I was on the phone with the dispatcher, I stated, "I am so sorry, but I think I may need the paramedics. I think I might have a heart attack."

When the paramedics arrived, they brought me into the ambulance and performed a full triage. To my surprise, everything checked out fine. The only issue was that my blood pressure was slightly elevated. They reassured me that I was okay and mentioned that it could have just been an anxiety attack. I remember thinking, "Anxiety attack?" It sounded so strange to me at the time because I had never experienced something like that before—or at least I hadn't recognized it as such. Around 3:30 a.m., I finally managed to calm myself down enough to get a couple of hours of sleep. I don't know how, but the next morning, I woke up and went to teach my usual three hours of fitness classes. It felt strange, especially considering what had just happened hours earlier. I carried on as if nothing had occurred, brushing it off like a 24-hour flu or something that would pass quickly. I even decided to take a rest day from my personal workout routine and assumed that a little downtime would be enough to reset.

Little did I know that this wasn't just an isolated event. It wasn't something I could just brush aside. This was the beginning of a journey with anxiety—something that, unbeknownst to me at the time, would follow me for the rest of my life. I continued with my life in San Francisco, and for a few weeks, I hadn't experienced another anxiety attack. It was now nearing Thanksgiving, a time I had been looking forward to for a while. I had scheduled time off to visit my family in Los Angeles—it was going to be the first holiday since I moved away, and I was excited to spend it with them. I remember booking my flight for a Thursday evening, but I still had to work that day.

My plan was to teach from 4 to 5 p.m. and then catch my flight around 6:30 or 7 p.m. That day, I walked into the studio with my bags packed, feeling energized and ready to go. I was excited because I knew that I'd be on my way home for a much-needed break with my family once the workout was over. As I prepared for the session, the technician was equally enthusiastic, though I felt a little bad for him. It was his first time running the studio independently, and I could sense his nerves. That day, it was just the two of us in the studio—him and me. I started the workout, and everything went smoothly. No technical issues, no hiccups—it all seemed perfect. I felt good knowing that in just a short while, I'd be heading home to spend the week with my loved ones.

Ten minutes into the workout, I felt a sudden chill up my spine. Almost instantly, I started seeing stars—flashes of light flickering all around me. My hands became shaky, and

I struggled to keep a grip on the weights. As the timer reset for the two-minute recovery period, I put on my most energetic voice, telling everyone on camera that I would grab my water off-camera and be right back. But behind that smile, I was feeling the most intense fear I had ever felt. I rushed out of the studio and into the technician's room, where my coworker was working. I told him, panicked, that I felt like I was about to faint and needed water. Without hesitation, he ran out of the room and upstairs to get me a cup of water. Meanwhile, I had no choice but to return to the studio because the timer was still running, and we couldn't cut the feed—it was a live class.

I jumped back on camera, continuing the workout as if nothing was wrong. The technician, seeing me back in action, left the water on the desk for me. Somehow, I managed to finish the 40-minute session and felt a little more like myself. But as I left the studio, I was confused, asking myself, "What is happening to me?" He handed me the water, and I drank it along with a snack or two, thinking maybe my blood sugar had dropped and I just needed to refuel. After that unsettling experience, I flew home to Los Angeles, trying to make sense of it all but not fully realizing what had just happened.

I spent the entirety of Thanksgiving with my family, and it was great—no anxiety attacks at all. I was able to hit the gym regularly, and we had an amazing time together. Everything felt normal, and I thought maybe the anxiety attacks were behind me. However, when I returned to San

Francisco, I experienced another anxiety attack while in the studio. Nothing provoked it; it just came out of nowhere. I usually have positive behavior, and I felt like I was starting to make some new friends in San Francisco. So, I couldn't understand why these anxiety attacks were developing. What was triggering them? At this point, the episodes were few and far between, but they were still unsettling.

A short while later, I returned to Los Angeles for three days to complete a certification that could only be done in person. While I was there, I met up with the person I had ended my relationship with. We made plans to go to lunch, and as he picked me up in his car, he showed me a project he was working on. He worked in production, and as I watched a video on his phone, I suddenly felt a wave of warm chills rush up my spine. I couldn't breathe properly, and no matter how I shifted my seat, I couldn't get comfortable. Assuming it was just low blood sugar, I waited until we got to the restaurant and immediately asked for apple juice or orange juice. I still felt cold and shivery as I drank it, almost like the chills you get when your body temperature drops, even though I had a sweater on. It was frustrating, and once again, I couldn't figure out why it was happening.

I pleaded with my ex to get our food to go and head back to his place because I couldn't stay in that restaurant or be in public at that moment. He was incredibly kind and understanding—he packed everything up, and we drove back to his house. Once there, he let me lie on his bed for about 45 minutes until I finally calmed down. Afterward, I drove home, exhausted, and slept as soon as I got there. I ended up sleeping for 14 hours straight. The anxiety had completely drained me both physically and mentally. Again, I was left confused, conflicted, and frustrated. I didn't understand why this was happening to me or where it was coming from. I'd always been relatively healthy—I worked out regularly, ate well, and cared for myself, aside from possibly consuming a little more caffeine than I should sometimes, but I never thought that could lead to something like this.

Back in San Francisco, I resumed my routine, and the anxiety seemed to settle down again. For about a week, the memory of that episode remained in my mind, but as I started feeling more like myself, it faded away, and there were no major issues. As the end of my lease approached, some of my coworkers began encouraging me to move to another part of town, particularly the East Bay in Oakland, where they lived. Oakland didn't have the best reputation, but it was starting to undergo many renovations and improvements, and they painted it as a great option for my next move.

My coworkers told me that moving to the East Bay would give me a better quality of life—more space and less expense compared to living in the city. So, I took their advice and began planning my move. During that time, I actually met someone romantically, and we went on a few dates. We can call him Will. Will lived in the East Bay, and it felt almost serendipitous—like everything was aligning. I was already planning to move to the East Bay, and now I had met someone who lived there too. It made me feel like maybe things were finally falling into place, and this was where I was meant to be. As with many decisions I had been making lately, I didn't have the input of my friends or family. I was navigating everything on my own, trusting my instincts, and making choices as I felt they were right for me. I started packing up my apartment, gearing up for the move.

Two days before I was set to move, Will flaked on dinner plans for that evening, and upon checking in on him, he called me and told me he was no longer interested in continuing the relationship. It was a sudden and unexpected blow. We had been dating for a little over a month, and I would check in periodically to see if we were both on the same page, leaning into my anxious attachment. I found myself facing yet another challenge just as I thought things were starting to settle. I felt absolutely crushed. I began questioning everything: Had I been fantasizing about the East Bay because of this person? Was that part of the reason I wanted to move? Even though my coworkers had convinced me it was a good decision, I started to confuse my motivations, wondering if my desire to move was tied up with my feelings for someone who no longer wanted to be in my life.

But despite those doubts, I reminded myself why I had made this choice. It was supposed to give me a better quality of life—more space and lower costs. The apartment I secured was brand new and bigger than my previous place in the city. I now had a two-bedroom apartment with separate office space, a modern kitchen, new appliances, and a washer and dryer in-unit. It felt like a major upgrade. I even brought my car up from Los Angeles, which had stayed behind when I initially moved. Things should have been looking up.

Once I got settled, I made a trip back to Los Angeles to pick up my car. I took the opportunity to enjoy time with friends and had a fun weekend in Palm Springs with my best friend. But when I returned to San Francisco, things took an unexpected turn. The morning after I arrived, I started feeling sick—congested, with what felt like allergy symptoms. I took a COVID test, and sure enough, it came back positive. Suddenly, I found myself locked inside my new apartment for five days, unable to work. During those five days, I experienced one of the worst panic attacks I've ever had. Later, my therapist told me it was a dissociative panic attack. If you're unfamiliar with that, it's when your mind tries to disconnect from reality, almost as a defense mechanism. My body didn't feel like it belonged to me—my arms, legs, even my reflection in the mirror. It was as if I was looking at myself, but it didn't feel like me. The sensation was terrifying, and I spiraled into complete panic.

I eventually managed to calm myself down and got through those five days of isolation before returning to work. However, the intensity of that experience made me realize it was time to seek professional help, so I decided to find a therapist. Although I had worked with therapists in the past, the experiences hadn't been great. One was recommended by my ex, who had been abusive, which understandably wasn't a positive experience. Another time, my mom took me to therapy when I came out to her, which also left me feeling uncomfortable. These encounters made me skeptical of whether therapy would work for me.

But this time, I was desperate. I signed up on a therapy website where they matched you with a therapist and began working with someone immediately. After my first session, I felt anxious for days. It was as though my entire body was vibrating, and I couldn't figure out why. I had talked through my feelings during the session, yet I still felt on edge.

Over time, that constant vibrating sensation started to fade, and I was able to live more normally for the next few weeks. What I find funny now, looking back, is that during that first month of working with a therapist, my anxiety hit an all-time high. But slowly, I began learning more about my anxiety and how to manage it. Seeing my therapist once a week started to feel like it wasn't enough. I had so much to unpack and process that the 50-minute session felt too short, like I needed to talk to them every day to maintain calm. That single session per week just didn't feel sufficient.

Over time, my therapist provided me with some tools to help me recognize and manage my anxiety. I still felt very much like a beginner handling it. As we continued our sessions, we discovered some significant things: Not only had I left my value system in Los Angeles, but I was also having an internal battle with what I was conditioned to learn and what I was trying to learn on my own. In San Francisco, I had no structure or sense of grounding. I realized I had become so reliant on the people in my life back in L.A. that I had lost the ability to rely on myself in the way I needed to grow. Remember, I grew up extremely sheltered and never ventured far as an adult. Over the next year, I worked through this realization with my therapist. I explored different modalities—meditation, self-soothing techniques, and even medication. I reached out to friends who had experienced similar struggles with anxiety, hoping to find solidarity or guidance. But despite all these efforts, I still couldn't find a solution to the problem. It felt like I was trying everything, but nothing was quite solving the underlying issue.

My journey through anxiety, therapy, and self-discovery in San Francisco has been anything but straightforward. What started as excitement for a new chapter in my life slowly became a challenge to understand and manage the anxiety that surfaced along the way. The realization that I had lost my value system and was overly dependent on the support network I left behind in Los Angeles, on top of unlearning some of what my family taught me, was a hard truth to face. However, it also became a critical part of my growth, and I was still learning and evolving well into my adulthood. During that year, I made some progress and experienced what felt like setbacks, but what remained was my persistence, which I needed as the following months unfolded with more stress than I was prepared for.

That November, I got a call from my parents regarding my cousin's health. A little backstory: My cousin on my father’s side was the youngest of three siblings. She was the last to marry, and on her honeymoon, she was diagnosed with cancer. She was treating it and was even said to be in remission. I spoke with her in April about life and planned to visit her. The call that followed was not good news. She had suffered a stroke, followed by a seizure, and they said the cancer was back and terminal. My mom said she might not make it to Thanksgiving, and I frantically looked for flights for my parents to go see her, as I couldn't leave at that time. They were able to visit, and I was idly waiting for updates. In between updates on her status, my mom would send me text messages with photos of my cousin's house as if it were a spectacle. I angrily told my mom that this was so inappropriate and completely wrong timing. I also received photos of my non-responsive cousin in my text thread. Devastated and angry, I connected with my therapist to vent my frustrations and fears. Having started journaling that year, I put my thoughts on paper, hoping that writing them down would alleviate my emotions. My cousin made it through Thanksgiving and even Christmas. But on January 2nd, 2024, she passed away. This girl, who I had grown up with and was only six years older than me, was gone. Her husband asked my brother and me to be the pallbearers at her funeral, and we immediately accepted. Through the last few months, as her health declined, we stumbled upon a new health issue within my own home. My dad was having bouts of dizziness and shortness of breath. He was in his 70s, so we had to get everything checked out. My dad was not one for going to the doctors after his history in hospitals, but he would go if we forced his hand. His blood panel came back a little abnormal, but we assumed he needed to change his diet.

On New Year's Day, my parents went to church, and I had brunch with some friends. I got a call from my mom during brunch, in which she stated my dad had collapsed in the church parking lot. They called the ambulance, and after a grueling 30 minutes, he was fine and went home.

My mom was very shaken and took action to schedule another appointment with the doctor, who wanted to run some extra tests. At this time, I was back in the Bay Area working, but I planned to be back in L.A. for my cousin's funeral. Coincidentally, that same weekend, my dad had an appointment with an oncologist. On that Friday morning, I drove my parents to the appointment, where we found out that my dad had Acute Myeloid Leukemia. Without processing it, I immediately took over the conversation and started discussing treatment options, life expectancy, and more. It was almost as if my parents were on mute, and I was the only one able to speak for them both. The shift in this dynamic with my parents could not have been more obvious to the doctor sitting across from me. My mom sitting there silent, my dad confused at the language that was being said. I was their only advocate. Knowing what my dad had gone through in the past, I chose the least invasive option for him to start chemotherapy. The fear of making decisions for my father without knowing their outcome overwhelmed me. This wasn't just choosing a food order for him without his input, this was truly life or death.

The next day after having made the first of many decisions for my dad's well-being, I laid my cousin to rest. It was a bittersweet, heartbreaking funeral filled with love and sadness washing over the ceremony. My parents could not make the drive, so I let them know they could stream the funeral. My dad could not bear to watch. His little niece, whom he had known since she was a child, was now gone and from the same illness he was now about to fight, though she had a different type of cancer, it was cancer all the same. After the service and the mercy dinner, we drove back to my parents to spend the day with them before my brother and I left for our respective homes. Upon getting home, I checked in with my parents to ask if they were able to stream the funeral. My mom immediately jumped in and said, "Your dad could not even listen to the funeral, so we turned it off". I connected with him shortly after, He did not make eye contact as we spoke.

I could hear his voice crack as he spoke about the funeral, with tears building up in his eyes. I sensed there was some fear for his future in his voice as he shared his sadness in his own way. On my drive back to Oakland, I felt a wave of sadness and stress. The following days weren't any better, they were filled with anxiety and negative dark thoughts. Not only was I stuck in the Bay for work, but now my dad was dealing with a life-threatening illness which was unfamiliar territory not only for me but for our family. I also carried the burden of having made all of the decisions to start his treatment, hoping I had made the right choice, trying to appeal to my dad's comfortability. As I felt a swirl of emotions, I remembered that I had a therapy session that week, which I was looking forward to.

My therapy session was in the morning, and I was getting my coffee to start my day. While making my cup of coffee, I started writing my dad's eulogy in my head, imagining the funeral and the sadness that would follow. I had just had a funeral, and gotten very bad news about my dad's health so it only made sense, but why did I have to go to such a dark place? As I shared this with my therapist, I started to choke up and cry. I feared that I had not spent enough time with my dad and that I had left him alone, with my mom unable to be there as any form of support. I felt like I was being selfish for having followed my dreams to this job in San Francisco. On top of that, I had planned a trip to London in February, and if anything were to happen while I was away, I would not be able to forgive myself. I slowly started to accept what was happening with my dad and proceeded to continue with my work life and personal obligations while checking in on him almost daily. I made an effort to drive down to Los Angeles once a month and stay for a few days to be with my dad during his chemotherapy and get some much-needed time away from San Francisco. By then, I was not in love with the city and was trying to figure out my permanent exit back to Los Angeles.

Eventually, the stress of commuting to Los Angeles started to become exhausting, all while navigating medication for my chronic anxiety and giving my all at work. If there was one thing I told myself, it was that I would not fold under life's challenges at work. Work was where I thrived, it was where my perfectionism was highlighted and the staff I worked with helped me work through my anxious moments when it felt uncontrollable.

My lease eventually came to an end, and my company was making some major shifts. They executed their third and biggest layoff since my hire. Thankfully, my position was not impacted, as they stated they valued my expertise and that I was a popular coach on the platform. They also allowed me to live in Los Angeles for the following months and commute up for work while we geared up for my dad's continued chemo treatments and stem cell transplant. Balancing my health, my dad's health, and maintaining a presence at work added a lot of pressure to my plate that I was not prepared for. I woke up with what felt like my body vibrating, my mind racing and me doing breathwork until I could not bear doing one more exercise. After months of treatment and hospital visits ee finally got my dad to a state of remission, and though we were all happy, we were not out of the woods yet. There was the matter of stem cell donation and transplant.

Prior to the transplant, the oncologist asked my brother and me to test if we were a match to donate. Being twins, we were both 50% matches. Given the history of familial responsibility, I was naturally expected to donate my stem cells, which required me to take an extra week off work for the process. My brother, who's schedule was monopolized by work and two children would not be able to take time away from his life to assist. I had a hard time accepting that given how much my parents had helped him over the years. But, eventually I accepted this responsibility as we received the results. I knew it would be a lot of stress on me, both mentally and physically, but I would do anything to help my dad stay healthy. If you're unfamiliar with that process, as the donor, I had to inject medication for five days to induce the growth of my stem cells for collection. I experienced some side effects, such as extreme bone aches and pains as my bones expanded to release new stem cells into my blood stream which would later be collected at the hospital. The collection day was nerve-racking, I went to the collection department and was placed on a bed. In one arm, they inserted an 18-gauge steel needle, which would remove blood from my body into the filtration system; another smaller needle would be placed in the opposite arm, where the filtered blood would reenter my body after the removal of my stem cells. This process took three hours. Upon completing my duty to my family, I went home. I couldn't help but feel frustrated. "Why me?" I asked myself. Why did I have to carry the burdens of my family? I felt even worse for feeling this way. On one hand, I had done an amazing thing; on the other hand, why didn't my parents put more pressure on my brother to contribute since he had been distant since my dad's initial diagnosis? This was a theme in my life: I, having to shoulder more responsibility while my brother got a "Get out of jail free card" time and time again. Followed by a phrase we say in Arabic "Haram" meaning to take pity on someone. I felt so frustrated whenever that was their default statement I wondered if there would be any pity left for me? But that was an obstacle I struggled to face head on with our family dynamic.

Once the stem cell donation was complete, it was time for my dad to begin receiving them. He would be under hospital supervision for at least a couple of months, so I was able to breathe a little easier knowing he would be taken care of. We walked him into the room and said good night just before he received his first round of chemo, but none of us were prepared for what was to come in the following weeks and months. During that time, while his immune system was low, he contracted pneumonia, which labored his breathing and left him bedridden and malnourished due to a lack of appetite. My dad went from being an independent person—driving himself to blood transfusions and being pretty content with where life had landed him—to barely being able to sit upright in bed without exhaustion, asking the nurses to put him out of his misery. This poor man was begging for relief. He looked at me and asked, "Massage?" I immediately jumped on his hospital bed, sat him up, supporting his back with my body, and proceeded to give him a shoulder and head rub to make him comfortable.

After a grueling couple of months, he was discharged and had to stay within close proximity to the hospital, which was about an hour's commute from home. Staying in a rehab facility each day was a new challenge, whether it was him fainting, refusing to eat, or having trouble doing daily tasks. My mom, having stayed with him at the rehab facility, left our home under my care. Balancing work in San Francisco, taking care of our pets and home, and making time to visit my parents to bring them necessities weighed heavily on my psyche.

I remember flying up on a Monday for work. I felt rattled with anxiety, worried about my dad's well-being. For a couple of days, I put on a show at work. The last place I wanted to be was in front of a camera, pretending to be okay. After that, I flew back down. Then, I had the responsibility of taking my dad to and from chemo. I found myself neglecting my own health, but the fear of losing my dad and not having given him enough time consumed my mind. At one point, I recalled driving straight to the rehab facility after barely touching down from San Francisco, only to be met with criticism from my parents for not bringing the right blankets or toiletries. I wanted to leave immediately and go home but felt guilty for feeling like I would be abandoning my family so I swallowed my pride and stayed until it was bed time. My anxiety was at an all-time high and was extremely unpredictable which added more stress to my day. One day, I was in the kitchen making lunch when I suddenly felt a sensation as if something had hit me on the head. I turned the stove off with food still in the pan. In a quiet panic, I walked to the couch and sat down, trying to collect myself. I checked my blood pressure which was high, my heart rate sped up and overwhelmed my body. I spend the remaining part of the hour self soothing to continue on with my day.

My anxiety started to manifest in strange physical experiences, like dizziness in random places or feeling foggy for the entire day. With the help of my therapist, I was able to combat my emotions and continue on with my routine as best as possible. My dad's health did not improve, so he was discharged to go home. When we arrived home, my job in San Francisco informed me that I could no longer work from L.A. They said I could not continue flying up as needed. I did not want to return to a city where I felt so out of place, but it was that or I would be out of a job. I discussed this with my dad, and he, in classic fashion, pushed me to go. I reluctantly signed a lease and planned my move back to the Bay Area while my dad remained in the care of my mom at home. I did my best to maintain a positive outlook on the situation, but it was challenging as my mom would call me frantic if something happened with my dad. My loneliness in San Francisco triggered more anxiety. I attempted to befriend my neighbor across the hall, and his friendship helped a lot. I grew close to him during my short time back in the Bay, but I still felt a void. My team at work felt disorganized and broken. I would barely see them, and when I attempted to make plans, they would dance around, giving me a direct no. I tried to take a trip to London to escape the stress, rationalizing that my dad’s situation at home made me want to be somewhere else. Unfortunately, London was not as relaxing as I had hoped. The trip was supposed to be just my cousin and me, as it had been the year prior. This time, he invited his sister, whom I love, and her fiancé, whom I equally enjoyed. But then there was another guest who became an unexpected liability. The whole week was filled with events, and I ended up managing this 22-year-old girl who seemed ungrateful for coming to Europe on someone else's dime. On top of that, my cousin, whom I was initially coming for, got himself into some trouble, making the whole week exciting and unpredictable in the worst ways. But it was in London, so I salvaged the trip as best as I could. I made sure to call my dad throughout to check on his progress.

I returned to the States to be met with the same anxieties I had left behind. I continued to focus on the things I could control, such as my nutrition, sleep, exercise, and putting effort into socializing to give my life more meaning in the Bay Area. It worked for a time, but then I would find myself right back where I had started. That April, we found out my dad's cancer had returned since the stem cell transplant was unsuccessful. I felt a strong sense of failure. All of that work, pain, and trauma for both my dad and myself seemed for nothing. He was now incapable of taking care of himself; he was weak and had to continue putting chemicals into his body. My sadness loomed over me, hanging on wherever I went. Some days, it felt like an out-of-body experience, and due to the stress, my body reacted by developing a rash on my nose. My anxiety was still there, and now I had a physical badge to show what the stress had created. After my dad's diagnosis, my health anxiety skyrocketed. Every strange feeling felt like something was seriously wrong with me. I would try to self-soothe, but that would only go so far before the feelings would return and take over.

It was May 31st. I was on my couch with a friend, watching television, when I received a call from my mother. She told me that my dad was being admitted to the ICU. She said there was fluid buildup in his body. He was battling an infection in his foot and had abnormal vitals. I knew something was wrong. I immediately emailed my job and called my human resources personnel, explaining that it was a family emergency. I told them that I needed to leave San Francisco right away to tend to my father. Without hesitation, she said, "Go take care of your family." I was afraid of seeming like I was abandoning my job, but my family always came first. I flew down to L.A. and immediately went to check on my dad. Upon arrival at the ICU, I could feel my anxiety heighten, and the sensation of dizziness began. Then, along came the priest to bless my dad—typically reserved for when things look bleak.

Over the following ten days, I drove to visit him, as he hated being alone in the hospital. Not surprisingly, he was not doing well. I would sit and chat with him, telling him my plans to move home or discussing fun topics like winning the lottery, which he enjoyed playing. The doctors finally decided they needed to remove the fluid from his body, as it was causing many complications for his heart rate and breathing. However, they faced a dilemma: they could not perform a less invasive procedure because laying him flat would put his heart in a compromising situation, so he underwent full surgery.

He came out of surgery, but due to his delayed recovery from anesthesia, they kept him intubated overnight. After he came to, we found that my dad could not swallow properly and was limited to IV nutrition, hoping he would regain his swallowing function. For an elderly person going under full anesthesia can be risky. If they cannot metabolize the anesthesia fast enough they may have to be intubated longer, in turn their swallowing mechanism may be impaired not allowing them to have any solid foods until they have regained control of swallowing properly. This is to prevent choking during food or beverage consumption. Father's Day rolled around, and I made sure to see my dad. His condition never changed, and he was still restricted to sucking fluid from a sponge at the end of a straw. He begged for sprite as it was his favorite soda. To lighten the mood I acted sneakily and soaked his sponge in soda and let him suck on it while saying “Shhh, don’t let the nurses see.” with a chuckle. His facial expression of exhaust didn’t change. As he was trying to enjoy his treat he started to cough from being unable to swallow. His mouth was covered with dry tissue and mucus, which made it hard for him to breathe. With the help of the nurse I was able to help alleviate some of the discomfort. I tried to remain strong for him, hiding my sadness with a joke and a smile. Little did I expect that Father's Day would be the last time I had a proper conversation with him. After that day he quickly declined, and keeping him awake was a challenge, as he would always fall back asleep mid conversation. His body was giving out and my mother, uncle, brother and I had to make a hard decision.

On June 19th, we made the decision with the doctors to stop his medication. On June 20th, we alerted the family that we were stopping the medication and that anyone who wanted to see him prior to that needed to be there. His room was filled with love from his brother and sister, my mom, brother, and cousins. At 12:30 PM, we stopped his meds and waited. In the midst of the tense wait the priest walked in to bless him before his passing. In classic fashion my mother pushed my brother and I to step outside to converse with the priest. Just beforehand my mother was pushing us to all take photos with my father while he was not conscious. I found that to be distasteful and with my added frustration, I did not understand why she would do that at such a critical moment and then push us to leave the room to talk to the priest. When I addressed this with her, she responded with "It's inappropriate to not sit with the priest and talk with him." With a slight smirk on her face. As if we had to entertain him for coming to my dad's bedside. My brother and I annoyed to leave my dad's bedside walked with the priest, my mother to the waiting room outside of the ICU and he proceeded to talk to us like children as if we had never experienced death before, while my mother sat idly by physically happy we were entertaining the priest to show we were a "good family". With annoyance I had stated that I had experienced enough death in my life to understand what was happening and the feelings surrounding the situation. Shortly after that statement, my cousin rushed into the waiting area and without a beat he frantically stated "It's happening!" My brother and I not caring about decorum immediately rushed out of the waiting area back into my dad's room. We watched as his breathing slowed and his consciousness faded. At 2:30, he took his last breath, and he was gone. Tears flooded my eyes as I held his lifeless hand, saying my goodbye.

During the last few months of his life, my life had a wild turn of events. Due to the excess stress that I was putting myself through to be as present as possible for my dad and family, juggling my presence at work, feeling guilty for having left my mother to handle my father alone and the uncertainty of my job in San Francisco my body started to react. On April 1ST, I noticed what looked like a small bump on the bridge of my nose. Seemed like the universe wanted to play a joke on me. But it felt like the only fool on that day was me for not knowing the signs. As the weeks progressed the bump turned into a rash that slowly started to take over my nose. In a panic I ran to my nearest dermatologist. She walked in, confident and crass. With barely even in inspection of my face she took one look and blurted out a diagnosis. "It's rosacea." In a monotone voice. I was confused. I have seen it on others before but never in a circular pattern as it laid on my face. She prescribed a strong steroid and sent me on my way. Confused about my diagnosis and annoyed at the doctor's bedside manner I followed instructions and placed the ointment on the infected area. Three days later, hoping it would have subsided it was more irritated than ever. I went back to the same office, but made sure to see a different doctor. This one thankfully seemed more empathetic to my situation. He gave me a different diagnosis, one that I was able to believe. He sent me home with more creams and a cleanser. I followed his instructions to a T. He said it would be weeks before my skin would go back to normal. As the weeks went on my rash started to change in form. Going from a bright red blotch on my nose, to a ring that went from nostril over the bridge to the other side. Frantically I facetimed my cousin in LA who is a doctor and she confidently confirmed it was a fungal infection and it needed time. It was not the end of May not much changed on my face, having had to use makeup to cover it's distant appearance on camera. But that was when I got the call about my dad. I immediately took time off work to tend to my father. While we were all there, I noticed that something on my face had changed. There was an odd tenderness on my lip but assumed it was dry skin. Days went by and I woke up with a swollen lip. It was more comical than it was scary. To paint a picture, it was as if I went to get lip filler, stopped halfway through the treatment and decided that it was enough. I took myself to the ER and was told it was a staph infection that needed antibiotics. Now I not only have a skin issue I was nursing, I, not had an infection on my lip, on top of my father in the ICU. Life really wanted to challenge me. Thankfully in infection subsided but the matter of my nose remained. Once again it changed form, mutating in front of my own eyes. It now became round rough patches on my upper nose and upper lip. Being I was at the hospital it coincidently was not far from my doctor in LA. I scheduled some blood work and explained to him what was going on. He drew my blood and let me know he would be in touch. Little did I expect that my news would come on one of the darkest days to note. The same day of my dad's passing, I received and email from the doctor office with my lab results. Now, having learned a lot about reading labs in the last year or so, I knew what to look for. Everything seemed normal except one result which I had never had before. It was suggested to me to get an autoimmune blood panel done, since my rash was persistent. My lupus blood panel came back positive, with my double strand DNA in the high zone. After meeting with a specialist, I was diagnosed with SLE, Systemic lupus erythematosus. Due to the stress of caretaking for my dad, being present for my family and trying to maintain a physical presence at work, my body reacted. While planning my dad's funeral, mourning his passing, I had to manage my already existing anxieties and now an unpredictable illness that will live with me forever.

I did not mean for this chapter to be consumed by my dad, but I wanted you, my reader, to understand the weight of the situation and it's impact on me and not only my mental health but my physical health as well. As someone in a home with high expectations its easy for stress to follow you like a shadow. Stress can be considered a silent killer, though you feel stress in many different ways, it is challenging to see the impact it has on your body until the damage is too far gone. Having lived in a stressful home I always thought that chaos was normal. I convinced myself that I thrived under pressure, which at times I did. This also lead to some procrastination on my end, needing that stress to kick me into high gear. What I failed to understand was that continuous amounts of stress put a strain on my long term health and well-being.

While managing my stress, health issues and now grief, I received an offer to move back to Los Angeles, where my new journey in an old place began. I was able to secure my goal of moving back to Los Angeles, unfortunately the person I was excited to move back for was no longer in my life. Though, Los Angeles is my familiar place, it didn't seem all too familiar. There was a new void where once it was filled, an old obstacle with a new challenge I need to face but I was not going to let my confidence waiver.

Therapy, while not always a quick fix, has been invaluable in helping me recognize and navigate my anxiety. Learning to rely on myself, experimenting with different coping mechanisms, and seeking advice from others who have faced similar struggles taught me that healing isn't linear, as much as we want it to be. It's a process of trial and error filled with setbacks and breakthroughs—moments of ease equaling moments of stress.

While I'm still on this path, I now realize that the tools and strength I need to rebuild my value system and manage my anxiety have always been within me. It's not about finding a perfect solution but about accepting the ongoing journey of self-awareness, resilience, and growth—embracing the journey rather than forcing yourself to reach the destination. As I embark on this new journey, having moved back to LA, I know I will face challenges and setbacks that will make me feel like I have started from square one, but that's part of life. So, as someone who has felt like I had it all figured out, only to look in the mirror and see an unrecognizable person, take the time to ask yourself, "Who am I? Who do I want to be? How can I get there?"

Chapter 7: What We Now Know

Anxiety and depression can be considered chemical imbalances in the human brain or a highly emotional state. Some choose to look at them from both lenses or one, and sometimes taking an emotional experience and turning it into a series of chemical events can lessen the impact it has on your mind, at least for me. During an anxiety attack, a complex game is played between different parts of the brain. Along with the amygdala and the prefrontal cortex, your brain releases hormones that can help you survive threats. This is your fight-or-flight response as your body releases adrenaline and cortisol. These hormones prioritize survival functions within the sympathetic nervous system, triggering the physical sensations and heightened awareness commonly experienced during an attack. Understanding these biological mechanisms can provide clarity and, for some, a degree of relief.

Though the symptoms can vary from one person to another, they are relatively similar: increased heart rate, shortness of breath, a body primed to move quickly, and a loss of the ability to perform other functions at that time. During depression or an extreme depressive episode, the brain experiences an overactive amygdala mis regulated by the prefrontal cortex, causing a negative cognitive bias. The nucleus accumbens, which resides in the brain's reward system, becomes dysfunctional, affecting the regulation of dopamine. The neuroplasticity of the brain can also become impaired, making it difficult to rewire the hippocampus, prefrontal cortex, and amygdala.

When I first experienced anxiety attacks and some depressive episodes, I immediately fell into the mindset of a scary emotional experience, feeling out of control and afraid of my own mind. I'm sure you may have experienced this as well. It's our fight-or-flight response; we are meant to be afraid in that state, just not when we are supposed to be enjoying the company of friends or watching television in the comfort of our homes.

Whether you look at it from a scientific perspective or an emotional one, one thing is certain: the experiences and emotions we face in childhood significantly impact how we perceive the world. From a young age, we start to learn how the world works through our family's view. This shapes us for better or worse. What I failed to recognize was that, although I seemed well-adjusted and unphased by those experiences as a young adult, they eventually rose to the surface when faced with adversity I had never encountered, manifesting as anxiety and panic attacks. Unprovoked and sometimes without a trigger, these feelings would spark up, and a fleeting fire would ravage my mind and body until it faded, leaving me feeling like a dried, stale shell of myself for a time. It took the will to work at it, unlearn what I was taught that no longer served me, and relearn what would best serve me. It sounds easier than it actually is.

For some, therapy is easily accessible, but for others, it isn't. Figuring out ways to improve your mental health, heal from trauma, and develop the toolkit to become a better version of yourself is important, but where do you start? Thankfully, with the help of my therapist, I came across worksheets and informative handouts that allowed me to better understand what I was feeling and what I needed to do to start unlearning the mindset I had acquired growing up. This is no easy task; when trying to unlearn a habit or thought process you have had for many years, just doing some of the work may not be enough. Just as your parents, significant others, and others reminded you of the rules or guidelines imposed on you, you have to do the same in the opposite direction for yourself. Remind yourself of the new value system you carry to push out the old. As someone with a systematic and rational mindset, it is important to note that when working on your mental health or unlearning bad habits, it's never fast nor linear. Be prepared for some successes and many more setbacks. But ultimately, you'll get to where you want to be.

When I was starting my journey to self-discovery, I did the cliché: "journal when you feel something" or even just put my thoughts on paper with no aim. I did not know how to begin other than to start writing.

Sure, that helped for a time, but it felt like it was improving my experience. I found myself rereading and reliving some of those scary moments, so I vowed not to reread what I wrote when I was done with my entry. Meditation was fine, but even with the right music or getting outside, I still felt lonely, and it did not relieve my anxiety attacks. The thing is, though working on your mental health is not linear in terms of progress, that also means there is no one way to cope with anxiety or depression, similar to medications that may be prescribed.

Medication was not my first line of defense. In fact, I frowned upon medication as I had heard horror stories about side effects and worsening symptoms of anxiety and depression. I tried for as long as possible not to use medication, but at one point, I felt desperate. When one medication did not work, I jumped on another. Each required a minimum of six weeks before I could determine if it was suitable for me. One medication caused my hormones and emotions to go haywire. I was easily agitated, to the point where an elevator moving slowly would set me off, and my body would vibrate with anxiety, but due to the medication, I was incapable of managing it. So I sat in anxiety until it just passed. My sleep was affected to the point where I would be awake at the buzzing in my head. Granted, at this time, my dad was undergoing chemo, and I had a lot on my plate.

When it comes to mental health and its tools, it's about trial and error; it's never a one-size-fits-all. But one thing is certain: if you develop a sense of self-awareness, you will be able to move through your experiences and become the happier, healthier version of yourself that you desire.

In this chapter, I wanted to give back to you, my reader. As I found in the self-help books I read about anxiety and depression, I had to sift through pages of text about someone else's experiences to figure out what I needed to start doing for myself, and even then, it did not feel clear. First, let's start off with some values. By understanding the values of our parents, the values of people we respect, and the societal values we hold to be true, we can then become aware of the values we currently live by and set goals for the values we want to embody. This exercise allowed me to tangibly see what values I had been raised with in contrast to the values I wanted to adopt and those I was currently holding. It was eye-opening to see that I had taken values from both of my parents, but only one remained dominant.

To build this exercise, start with six squares in two columns. In the first two pairs of squares, list three values from each parent. In the second pair of squares below, add three values of someone you respect and the societal values you believe to be true. In the last set of squares, write down the values you aspire to live by and those you are currently living by.

Mother's Values	Father's Values
1.	1.
2.	2.
3.	3.
Values of someone you respect	Values of Society
1.	1.
2.	2.
3.	3.
Values you Aspire to have	Values You Currently have
1.	1.
2.	2.
3.	3.

If finding your values seems challenging, you can use a value ranking worksheet online. The concept is to rate the values listed from 1 to 10, with one being the highest ranking on your list of importance and ten being the lowest. Some of these aids can help spark ideas when you don't know where to start.

For me, the hardest part was ranking my values, as I found all of them important, and I'm sure you may face the same dilemma. Think of this exercise as if you are looking for an apartment. You are the apartment, and the values are the amenities you desire. What are the ten things you need in your apartment? Could that be a dishwasher, washer, dryer, fireplace, parking, etc.?

Now, out of the ten things you need in your apartment, what are the four things you absolutely cannot live without? What are three things you could be indifferent to, and what are three things you could be alright without having?

Treat your values as such. What are four values you know you want in your life? Three that you feel indifferent about, and three that don't hold significant importance but would be nice to have? Once you have figured out your value system, it would be ideal to look at your boundaries. Growing up in an immigrant household, there never seemed to be any boundaries other than the ones my parents set. My parents didn't believe in privacy, and some of the boundaries they set didn't seem to hold any logic. It felt more like a power play. This stunted my ability to speak up for myself and effectively set and maintain boundaries with family, friends, partners, and work.

Setting boundaries can be challenging, especially when you get frustrated and have an emotionally charged situation due to a lack of boundaries. In this exercise, you can become more aware of how good you may be at setting boundaries and develop ways to improve them. First, write down a few experiences where you felt challenged in setting boundaries. Next, write down how you would typically handle or respond to those situations. Once you have written those responses down, write down how you could better handle them with your adjusted response to that specific situation. By doing this, you can better train yourself to respond in a more confident, pragmatic way rather than through emotional explosions or, conversely, by saying nothing and letting others dictate your boundaries.

The misconception when you are new to setting boundaries with friends or family is that you are being mean, unaccommodating, difficult, etc. For someone who is not versed in setting boundaries, it may seem awkward at first, and you may even feel guilty for being concerned about how others may perceive you.

In some cases, you may have individuals in your life who make passive-aggressive comments when they do not get their way or if you start setting boundaries. As someone whose parents always made passive-aggressive comments that sparked guilt, frustration, and other unsavory emotions, which would ultimately result in an emotional explosion, I then became the villain. I had to—and am still learning—not to be triggered by passive-aggressive statements.

In this next exercise, you can use your experiences, or look up scenarios to practice. First, find a situation that can be an inconvenience to you or something that was done unfairly. Write down three different counter statements: one that is passive-aggressive, one that is aggressive, and one that is assertive. You can do this with as many scenarios as you see fit. The goal of this exercise is to learn the differences between the three and to practice being assertive without being aggressive. This can also help you set boundaries in a firm way rather than exploding out of frustration, as some of us, including me, have done many times, which does not lead to a successful outcome.

When we get frustrated and let our emotions get the best of us, our prefrontal cortex activity decreases, making it difficult to think before we act, which leads to a couple of things. First, it makes logic take a back seat, which can cause unexpected verbal or physical outbursts. Secondly, when we are frustrated or angry about something, we may not be able to properly articulate the issue and immediately jump into blaming.

When tension rises between two individuals or within a group, and someone with a boundary being crossed reaches their tipping point, using blame phrasing can escalate the conflict. Phrases like “You did this” or “You always say that” tend to put the other person on the defensive, making them less receptive to hearing about the boundary that was crossed and more resistant to resolving the issue. This makes it harder to effectively communicate and set boundaries.

Practicing "I statements" is a constructive way to navigate these situations. "I statements" allow you to clearly express what you are feeling, what you need, and how the situation is affecting you without assigning blame. For example, instead of saying, “You never listen to me,” you might say,

"I feel unheard when I try to share my thoughts." This shifts the focus from accusing the other person to expressing your own emotions and needs, encouraging a more open and productive dialogue. For me, practicing "I statements" consistently helped me gain confidence without arrogance, enabling me to share my feelings and needs compassionately but assertively. It allowed me to address situations with clarity and respect, even in moments of heightened emotion. However, it's important to acknowledge that even with practice, it's not always easy. To this day, I sometimes catch myself falling back into blame phrasing when frustration gets the better of me. Recognizing this tendency helps me correct my course and continue improving. Communication is a journey, not a destination, and progress is what matters most.

At some points, I would ask myself: "What am I doing all of this for?" I was blinded by the fear that I would not be able to feel like my confident self before developing anxiety. That is when my therapist gave me a tool that helped put perspective on what I was feeling and why I was doing all this work. It is titled the Life Story Exercise.

First, you start by writing about your past—who you were and the challenges you faced and overcame. Take as much space as you need to explore this part of your journey. The second part should focus on your present: who you are now, how you have changed from your past self, and the current challenges you are navigating. This is an opportunity to reflect on your life as a whole rather than focusing on one specific situation. Lastly, write about your future. Consider how you envision yourself growing and changing from who you are now. What will your life look like in the future? If you ever feel stuck in the moment or experience negative emotions, you can look back at your past to remind yourself of the obstacles you have overcome. The goal is to create a complete picture of your life—past, present, and future—and your aspirations, allowing you to shift focus from any one negative experience to the bigger picture of your journey and potential.

We need to understand that depression often stems from being unable to move on from the past, dwelling on the bad things that have happened. Anxiety, on the other hand, is rooted in fear of the future and its uncertainties, preventing you from living in the present. Breaking free from these negative thought patterns helps you view your life through a broader lens instead of focusing on a narrow, magnified perspective.

I once came across a video as I was doom scrolling on social media that deeply changed my view on depression. In it, a woman asks a man why she feels depressed all the time. The man responded with a question of his own: "Do you know the definition of depression?" When she said no, he explained that depression could be seen as "compression." He described compression as a state where you withdraw from society to search for answers that the world around you cannot provide. When you fail to find these answers externally, you turn inward, seeking them within yourself.

This inward journey, while isolating, allows you to emerge as a more enlightened version of yourself. It is an experience of growth and self-discovery, one that can occur multiple times in life. By going through this experience with negative emotion, it feels like depression. By reframing it as an opportunity for growth, it becomes a transformative experience. It's important to note that not all depressive feeling can be considered compression as depression looks and feels different for everyone. Some may be clinically depressed and in need of professional intervention, while some may feel moments of depression and can easily bounce back after some time away from society.

Of course, looking inward isn't easy. I know this from experience. There were days when I was afraid to be alone with my thoughts, and this fear would sometimes trigger panic. Panic attacks can feel overwhelming and terrifying, making it hard to think clearly or feel in control. It can seem as though you're in the backseat of your mind, unable to regain control. During a panic attack, your nervous system goes into overdrive. Your body releases fight-or-flight chemicals—like adrenaline and cortisol—that are meant for life-or-death situations, not for moments when you're simply trying to relax at home or enjoy time with friends in a safe environment. It's crucial to troubleshoot your nervous system and redirect its focus during these moments.

When you're not in the middle of an attack, assessing your panic can be helpful. Many online resources or PDFs are available to help you evaluate the symptoms, difficulty, and severity of your panic attacks. Understanding your triggers can empower you to prepare for future episodes. When you're in the middle of a panic attack, however, there are several techniques that can help:

Cold Showers or Ice Packs: Applying cold sensations to your neck or body can quickly calm your nervous system.

Tapping Method: Redirect focus by tapping on your chest or another part of your body. This physical sensation can help ground you.

Sour Candies: The intense sourness shifts your attention to the sensation, reducing the overwhelming feelings of panic.

Physical Activity: Engaging in work or exercise can redirect your energy and give your mind a productive focus.

Some of my friends who suffer from anxiety have suggested putting that nervous energy into something constructive, such as completing tasks or exercising. This helps shift the focus from your thoughts to the activity at hand.

Anxiety and panic attacks can feel debilitating, but it's important to remember: it's your body, and you are in control—even when it feels like you're not. With the right techniques and mindset, you can manage these experiences and gradually reclaim your sense of calm and balance.

When dealing with depression or experiencing depressive episodes, the key is to take action—just get up and move. It doesn't matter what you do: complete a daily task, go for a walk, paint, work out, or engage in any other activity. The focus isn't on understanding why you're doing the task but simply on doing it. Depression often feels overwhelming and helpless, as though there's no resolution to the issue at hand. But sometimes, the answer lies in giving yourself time to feel, process, and reflect. This time allows you to think, rewrite your narrative, or take steps to prevent similar experiences in the future. It's all about how you perceive your depression. By shifting your perspective, as mentioned earlier, you can begin to view your struggles not as permanent obstacles but as opportunities for growth and understanding. Movement, no matter how small, is a step toward progress.

As someone who isn't a clinical psychologist but has deeply explored the intricacies of mental health and illness, I recognize that chemical imbalances can play a role in mental health for some individuals. However, no definitive studies accurately quantify how much of the U.S. population suffers from such imbalances. If you're curious about this, seeking professional help can provide a clearer understanding of your brain's chemistry. Personally, I invested in a genetics test to better understand which mental health medications might work most effectively with my body's chemistry. While this didn't directly change my mental health status, it provided valuable insights and increased my awareness should I decide to revisit the option of medication in the future. Interestingly, the test revealed that I have a genetic mutation that prevents my body from properly breaking down folic acid. Upon further research, I discovered that over 40% of the U.S. population has this MTHFR gene mutation, which can reduce folate uptake and potentially exacerbate anxiety-like symptoms.

Whether you're working on rewiring your own behaviors or helping others develop new habits, the key to success lies in repetition. Consistently practicing and reinforcing these changes is essential for creating lasting transformation, both within yourself and in your interactions with those around you.

Growing up as a product of immigrant parents is an unparalleled experience. Though there may be some similarities from culture to culture, each family has a different set of rules and guidelines, whether healthy or not. Each experience will be different for everyone because these experiences are never one size fits all. As I have had to learn when working on myself, there is no systematic way to work through anxiety or depression. But the ability to be aware of its presence and unhealthy behavior and your response to that behavior. For me, this epiphany came later in life, and I did not start digging until I had my episodes of panic/anxiety attacks.

Children of immigrants often find themselves straddling two worlds—the traditional world of their parents and the modern world of their peers. This duality can lead to internal conflicts and the challenge of forming a cohesive identity. It may involve reconciling different languages, customs, and social expectations. While this experience can be challenging, it also has the potential to foster adaptability, empathy, and a broader worldview. The journey of an immigrant child is rarely straightforward. It involves constant negotiation between different cultural expectations, personal aspirations, and family obligations. This process of navigation can be both enriching and challenging, often leading to a unique perspective on life and identity. It's important to recognize that there is no "correct" way to experience this journey—each individual's path is valid and worthy of respect.

For many of us, products of immigrant parents, the pressures of balancing cultural expectations with personal aspirations can contribute to many challenges, specifically, for the sake of this book, anxiety and depression. These issues may be exacerbated by cultural stigma surrounding mental health or a lack of understanding within the family unit. Recognizing these challenges is a crucial first step in addressing them effectively. Though I have started to better understand myself, nurturing my inner child, which I repressed for so many years, still takes work and reminds me that this journey is ever-changing. Now that I have the tools and the confidence I lacked before, this continued journey of self-discovery is not as scary as it used to be. I started the process of writing this book in anger and frustration toward my situation, but I completed it with more love for my family. We love them for how much they truly invested in their family and the desire to make sure they set us up for success, and with that love comes compassion and empathy. Compassion for what they had gone through to get into this country and empathy for how they were raised is all they knew. I've learned that my growth did not diminish my love for my parents but allowed me to learn how to walk next to them in my own way rather than drowning in their shadows.

Remember that, deep down, we are all innocent souls, though wrapped in layers of challenges, trauma, fears, and habits we've developed over time. By taking steps to understand our traumas, triggers, and bad habits, we can begin the process of unlearning what has been conditioned in us and relearning how we want to live and be. This journey requires letting go of the past, staying grounded in the present, and actively shaping the future we desire. It's about reclaiming our authenticity and choosing growth over stagnation.

Made in the USA
Middletown, DE
08 February 2025